Out
OF THE
Ordinary

*Awareness of God
in the Everyday*

PETER VERITY

Liguori

LIGUORI, MISSOURI

First published by Darton, Longman and Todd, London, UK, 1997

Library of Congress Cataloging-in-Publication Data

Verity, Peter.
  Out of the ordinary : awareness of God in the everyday / Peter Verity — 1st ed.
    p. cm.
  ISBN 0-7648-0213-5
  1. Cathloic Church—Prayer-books and devotions—English.
2. Spiritual life—Catholic Church. 3. Bible. N.T. John—Meditations. I. Title.
BX2182.2.V47 1998
242—dc21   98-11998

Bible quotations are taken from the Jerusalem Bible, published and copyright 1966, 1967, and 1968 by Darton, Longman & Todd Ltd and Doubleday and Company, Inc.

Printed in the United States of America
02 01 00 99 98 5 4 3 2 1
First Edition

For my Mum and Dad,
who first instilled in me
a sense of wonder and awe.

Contents

Acknowledgments

Over the years, I have been personally strengthened in my faith and prayer through contact with the Christian Life Community (C.L.C.). The spirituality of C.L.C., which is based on Saint Ignatius of Loyola and united to a worldwide network, is particularly appropriate for a busy lifestyle. When I worked in London for several years, the regular fortnightly meeting with a small group of people to share where God had been in our lives and to reflect together on the Scriptures was a source of great help. The suggestions for personal prayer and for a listening group in this book are based on C.L.C. literature. I am indebted to them for this material and also for the help which C.L.C. members have given me over many years in my personal journey of faith.

Introduction

The world is full of revelations about God. These are not usually in the dramatic events of life. They are very close to us, in our hearts and in the ordinary things in our world. If only we had the time and the desire to discover them, how much richer our lives would be! And how much richer our world would be if we shared our stories with other people.

There is a lovely quotation from *In the Springtime of the Year* by Susan Hill:

> Yet even as a small child, she had not believed, as others did, that heaven was in the stars, up and up above her, for there was something that frightened her in the night sky, a coldness, with only air rushing through the dark spaces between. No, she had always sensed that heaven was no further away than the tips of her own fingers, and if she were given eyes to see, it would be there, all about her and astonishingly familiar. She felt it now. If she reached out....

This book is about the adventure that a journey to discover God can be. In these pages, I tell some stories from my own personal experience. They are not big sensational stories but everyday ones. I try to show how it is in the ordinary that we learn about ourselves, about God, and about God's dealings with us. I hope to encourage you to do the same yourself.

There are three fundamental beliefs underlying what I have written in this book. First, I believe that we need to use our imagination more in prayer. This can be somewhat threatening because imagination can lead to false flights of fancy, in which our feet leave the ground and we become removed from reality. This need not be so if we realize that the product of our imagination should not be regarded as "gospel" truth and must be kept in perspective. In this book I have used my imagination to say, "God is like...." This is not a doctrinal statement and must not be judged as such. It is a way of exploring the mystery of God and of deepening our awareness of God's presence. I believe we could all benefit in prayer by using our imagination more, and by allowing ourselves some dreams of what God might really be like. I hope my use of imagination in this book will encourage you to look into your own experience, to use your imagination, and to find your own images to describe God's presence in your life.

The second fundamental belief underlying this book is that our ordinary human experience is valuable and important and that it is in this experience that we meet God. People sometimes put their prayer into a separate compartment, keeping it for set times (e.g., Sundays) or particular places (e.g., a church). Within the story of each of us there are experiences and incidents that can point us to God. More often than not, it is in the small everyday events that we find the sudden awakening of a new intuition. If the telling of my experiences encourages even one person to look afresh at his or her immediate surroundings to discover some new insights into the mystery of God, then this book will have accomplished what is intended.

Finally, underlying much of what I have written is the belief that we all need to develop an awareness of the God who is deep within us. To regard God as distinct from us and outside us, whom we meet face-to-face as a separate person, seems to me to limit our prayer and our understanding of God. The approach I have taken in this book is to try to be aware of the God who is within us and then to see what are the consequences of this for our faith. This is not a question of either/or, rather a both/ and. But I hope this method may help to expand your awareness of God and may overcome some of the difficulties many people find in relating to a God who can seem at times to be invisible and rather detached from our experiences.

Saint John's Gospel

It is quite by chance that the Scripture reflections chosen for each chapter come from Saint John's Gospel. When I was writing the book, it just happened that the most appropriate passages for each theme seemed to come from that gospel. As the ideas developed, I found myself noticing this and wondered why it might be. Perhaps there are two principal reasons.

In the first place, three key words occur frequently throughout this gospel: *seeing, believing,* and *knowing.* They are almost technical words that need putting in quotation marks or in capital letters. They describe the process of faith according to Saint John and are a model for all growth in faith.

According to Saint John, the first stage in all faith is seeing or experiencing a situation. "Come and see" was the invitation to the first disciples. The invitation to see and pay attention to our experiences is given to us, too, and is the first step in our faith journey. This "seeing" leads on to belief, which involves an act of commitment. At the end of the teaching about the "bread of life" in chapter 6 of Saint John's Gospel, people are given a choice—to believe or to walk away. In the same way, as the second important step in our faith journey, all of us are called to make a positive commitment to God, usually within the context of a believing community. If the positive choice to believe is made, this in turn draws us into the third and final stage of "knowing." This is the essence of John's contemplative faith. His gospel is a manual for the final stage of Christian initiation, which is knowing God's wisdom and beholding God's glory.

So the essence of faith in Saint John's Gospel is *seeing* a situation, *believing* in the God who is present in it, and finally coming to *know* God fully. It is succinctly summed up at the end of the gospel: "These [signs] are recorded so that you may believe that Jesus is the Christ, the Son of God, and that believing this you may have life through his name" (John 20:31). Those who are familiar with the Cardijn "See-Judge-Act" method of reflection will recognize many similarities here.

The other reason why Saint John's Gospel is particularly appropriate for this book is that John constantly uses outward physical "signs" to explain and lead us to an inner spiritual reality. In this sense it is a gospel that can be described as "sacramental." Sacraments have been defined as "outward signs of inward grace." In his gospel, John explores many of the signs of salvation in the Old Testament—manna, water, desert, the temple, and so on—and shows how they all point to Jesus. He leads us to "see" and reflect on these signs; to "believe" that Jesus is the final embodiment of all the hopes of the people of Israel; to "know" that Jesus is the new covenant between God and his people. John also adds new signs. Jesus is light, life, truth, vine, shepherd, door, king. In the physical reality of Jesus, the "flesh," John discovers the reality of God.

As you read this book, I hope that you, too, will follow the pattern—"seeing" your own experience and recognizing that experience to be in some sense "sacramental"; making an act of faith and commitment to the God who is present in that experience; and finally coming to "know" and understand God better than before.

How to Use This Book

First and foremost, this book can be used for personal spiritual reading and prayer. To read a paragraph or a page slowly two or three times, and use that for prayer, may be more beneficial than settling down to a long read! Each chapter begins with something from my own experience. These are simple things—a radio, a lighthouse, the sea, and so on—which, with a little imagination, can describe something about God and God's presence around and within us. At the end of each chapter there is a short section, "For Personal Prayer." This is meant to help you as an individual to move into prayer on the theme of the chapter. It includes a Scripture passage from Saint John's Gospel and some points to help your reflection. In some cases, when the full Scripture passage is too long, I have indicated this and suggested you use a Bible to read the full version. More detailed information on how to use each chapter for prayer is given below.

The examples given in each chapter come from my own experience, which is within the Christian tradition. For this reason, some of my comments and applications will be most easily accessible to people with the same background. However, I have tried to show how the underlying spiritual principles are universal and, although explained in Christian terms, can be accepted and taken up by people of other faiths too.

As well as being used for personal prayer and spiritual reading, I hope that this book can be taken up by groups from parishes and organizations. It is important to share our stories with others, for in this way we expand our own and others' ideas about God. Telling stories and listening to them builds up a wonderful and complex kaleidoscope, an ever-expanding picture of the wonder of God's love. The themes in this book could be the starting point for groups to share their stories. I have suggested this might be done through a "listening group" rather than the more familiar discussion group. Suggestions as to what this means and how to do it are given below, and there is a reminder about them at the end of each chapter.

Listening groups made up of people from different Christian traditions will be of particular benefit, because hearing our varied experiences brings us closer together. When we share our stories, we will find ourselves standing shoulder to shoulder, supporting one another and helping one another in our common task, which is to grow into the fullness of Christ. Those involved in RCIA (the Rite of Christian Initiation of Adults) in parishes may also find this book helpful. It is not a textbook for RCIA, nor is it a course. But because it is about a journey of faith, it may resonate with people who are in the process of reflecting on their own journeys. As background reading, therefore, it should help to expand on the existing RCIA literature.

Suggestions for Personal Prayer

General Points

First of all, decide where you are going to pray. It's good to have a special prayer place, quiet and comfortable, even if it is just a corner of your bedroom or your living room. Make sure your prayer place helps you to pray. For example, you will probably find it easier to pray sitting down—but make sure your chair isn't too cozy or you just might fall asleep! Some people find it helpful to have a candle to focus on, and you may want to ensure that your Bible is handy.

Then decide when to pray. Try to put aside at least fifteen minutes when you won't be interrupted (take the phone off the hook) and try to stick to that time, however difficult it may be at first. Be realistic about choosing your time. For example, if you are not a "morning" person, don't try to get up early to pray—you'll just end up concentrating on keeping awake.

Keep a bookmark in this page and one in the chapter you are using for prayer. This is so that you keep an eye on the suggested pattern for prayer and can also find the Scripture passages and questions for reflection at the end of each chapter.

A Pattern for Personal Prayer

1. **Becoming aware of God's presence.** When you begin your prayer time, light your candle as a sign of prayer and start by trying to be still. Just sit quietly for a minute or two. Put aside anything you are worrying

about and simply remember that God is with you, even if you find it difficult to feel his presence. If you are not used to being still, you may find that this takes quite a long time. Ask God to help you in this prayer time.

2. **Asking for what you want.** When you have become still and relaxed, ask God for what you want from this particular prayer time. (Some people call this a "grace.") In each chapter I offer a suggestion as to what this might be—though you may discover that you want to ask for something quite different.

3. **Scripture and points for reflection.** Next, slowly read the suggested Scripture passage and commentary. Stop reading if anything strikes you, and just stay with it until you want to go on to the next bit. Or you may find that you want to read the passage two or three times and then go back to the phrases that seemed to stand out for you. The questions to help reflection are intended to focus your attention on certain issues arising from the chapter. Use whatever you find helpful in these, and don't worry if some of the questions are not helpful.

4. **Talking with God.** Before it is time to end your prayer, put this book aside and spend some time talking to God the Father, or Jesus, or the Holy Spirit. Talk about how you felt as well as what you thought. You may want to refer to the particular grace you asked for, or you may simply want to thank God for everything he has done for you. When you are ready to move out of your prayer, end with an Our Father or Glory Be.

5. **Looking back over your prayer.** Afterward, jot down a few notes about your prayer. This will be especially

useful if you are going to share in a group, but many people keep a private prayer diary just for themselves, and you may like to try this. Note how you felt in the prayer and what you were thinking about. Don't try to remember everything, just ask God to help you recall whatever he wants you to remember.

Suggestions for a Listening Group

General Points

Many people are familiar with discussion groups. But discussion groups sometimes become a kind of battle, in which the strongest people manage to say most and the quiet people hardly have a chance to speak. Sometimes in discussion groups people simply wait for a chance to get their oar in, and so do not hear or understand what the other person is saying.

What I would like to suggest here is a different kind of group, one in which most of the time is spent listening to what God is saying through other people rather than in talking. For this you will need at least three other people, although a group of five to seven is probably best. If there are ten of you, split into two groups.

Arrange the chairs in a circle and take the phone off the hook. You may find it helpful to have a candle on a small table in the middle of the group. Ask someone to "lead" the group. This means keeping an eye on the time and being responsible for making sure that no one interrupts anyone else or comments on what another person has said. (Take turns doing this so that no one is burdened with the job each time.) If you are going to have a cup of tea after the meeting, don't interrupt things to put the kettle on. It won't hurt to have a bit of a gap while you wait for it to boil!

Before You Meet

One element that is absolutely essential if these groups are to be successful is that each member of the group must have spent some time using the passage of Scripture for personal prayer before coming to the group. This is necessary as preparation because the purpose of the group meeting is to listen to what has happened in each person's prayer time. If members of the group start getting lazy about this, the group will soon become ineffective.

A Pattern for a Listening Group

1. **Becoming aware of God's presence.** At the beginning of the meeting, the group leader should light the candle and invite people to be still for a minute or two. It is helpful for the leader to use a watch to ensure that this time isn't cut short. The leader could suggest that everyone try to become aware of God's presence in the group.
2. **The grace and the Scripture.** The leader reminds the group of the grace for which they were asking during the prayer time. (Each chapter suggests what to ask for.) Then another member of the group reads aloud the Scripture passage that was used in the personal prayer.
3. **Silence.** The leader should tell everyone that there will now be five minutes of silence in which to recall the

personal prayer time and that he or she will say when the time is up. In this silence some people may want to refer to the notes they made—but it is best if these are not read aloud in the sharing time.

4. **Sharing and listening.** This is the time to take turns speaking. The important thing is that you simply listen to one another—don't interrupt and don't comment on what anyone else is saying. You may need to remind one another of this as it is very easy to forget. The leader should invite someone to start sharing. When they have finished, leave a moment or two of silence before the next person starts to speak.

5. **Deepening the reflection.** When everyone has had a chance to speak, you may want to have a second round of sharing. You could invite people to think about the church, parish, or group to which you all belong and to reflect on its life. Although this second round of sharing can become more of a discussion, see if you can keep to the practice of listening to one another without interrupting or telling someone else that they are wrong. Make sure that everyone gets a chance to speak a second time if they want to.

6. **Closing the meeting.** At the end of the group meeting, spend a moment or two in silent prayer before saying the Our Father or Glory Be together.

Out
OF THE
Ordinary

1
Conversion and Repentance–
The Dawning of Awareness

God is present everywhere, within us and about us. To become aware of such a presence deep in our being, we need to go through something of a conversion experience. In this chapter, I have used the idea of the dawn as a suitable way to describe how the awareness of God's presence grows and develops in our lives.

Most people rarely see the dawn. Exceptions might include taxi drivers, shift workers, bus and train drivers, postal workers, and newspaper deliverers who see the dawn in the course of their work. Holiday-makers, too, on cheap, middle-of-the-night flights will often see the dawn on their way to and from their sunshine resort.

My most memorable experience of the dawn is rather dramatic. It took place on the Mount of Moses in the Sinai Desert in Egypt. This was during a field trip when I was doing a sabbatical study in Jerusalem. We had traveled overland and camped a few miles from the Mount of Moses. At about 3:00 A.M. we crawled sleepily out of our tents and climbed into Land Rovers to take us to the foot of the mountain. The plan was to make the ascent in the dark. With only the light of the stars to show us the way, we climbed about three thousand feet in the cold, crisp air. A few hundred feet below the summit of the mountain we stopped. In the silence that precedes great events, we awaited the first signs of dawn.

If you have ever waited for the dawn, you will know that it is impossible to pinpoint the exact moment at which it begins. For quite some time, as you peer at the sky to see if there is any change in the light, the question remains: "Is this it or do we have to wait still longer? Perhaps this is only imagination or the light of the stars?" Then, very slowly, it becomes obvious that, even though it is impossible to see the difference from one moment to the next, the dawn really is starting to happen at last. As the minutes tick by, blackness changes to deep purple, which slowly merges into every possible shade of reds and oranges, greens and browns. And then a whole new world materializes as the contours of the land become clearer and as more and more detail emerges. It is as though a mighty artist were filling in the colors to complete a beautiful painting or as if an embroiderer were weaving in more and more colored threads to execute an exquisite tapestry. Every living thing seems to hold its breath at this daily miracle of creation, waiting for the moment when the bustle of daily life can once again begin.

Scripture says that God's presence in our lives is like the dawn. In the Benedictus, the prayer of Zechariah before the birth of John the Baptist (Luke 1:67–79), we are told (in the Grail version) that God is the one "who visits us like the dawn from on high." This is a beautiful description of God's presence in our world and of how we become aware of it.

It is easy to say, "God is present everywhere." It is much harder to begin to understand what this really means and to become conscious of God's presence. God is present, not simply as the one who made all things, but more important as the one who is at the heart of everything. It is as though God holds the whole of creation in one great embrace. There is nothing outside this embrace and, therefore, nothing outside God. Just as the dawn touches, embraces, and transforms everything on the face of the earth, so it is with the God who "visits us like the dawn from on high."

Included in this embrace of God in a very special way is each and every human person. Deep within the heart of everyone there is an eternal echo of the Divine. This is true of all human beings, not just those who are adherents of a particular faith or religion. Many people have a sense of this eternal echo, often without recognizing it as such or being able to name it. For many it will be experienced as a longing for something that transcends reality. Those who have a religious faith may describe it as the presence of God, while people with no attachment to any faith will be conscious of a sense of wonder or beauty or awe.

One of the reasons why people so often fail to explore this sense more deeply is that they simply take it for granted and do not recognize the beauty and potential of it all. I love the story of the teacher who asked her class, "Which is more important, the sun or the moon?" After some thought, one little boy put his hand up and said, "Obviously the moon is more important because it shines and gives light when everything is dark. The sun is less important because it shines when it is daylight!" Just as we take daylight for granted, so we often fail to notice the gentle presence of God in our world and deep within our hearts.

But whether we are conscious of them or not, the embrace of God for everything in creation and the echo of the Divine deep within the heart of everyone are part and parcel of our existence. Like the "dawn from on high," God touches and permeates everything on the face of the earth. To be conscious of these realities and respond to them positively puts us in closer harmony with our true nature and destiny and brings new life, hope, light, and color to our lives. If you have ever watched a new day beginning, you will have noticed that as the first shadows begin to emerge, everything, such as the shape of the hills or the silhouette of a tree, appears to be black and white and can be seen only in outline. Only as the dawn progresses do the colors start to come to life, until the light of day reveals them in all their splendor. When we become conscious of God's presence, the black-and-white outline of our lives will gradually take on new meaning and color. It will certainly mean a new day and a new creation for each of us when we become aware of the gentle and sure touch of God on the fabric of our lives.

The word *conversion* comes to mind as an appropriate way of describing this process of growing awareness. Many people think of conversion as a change from one faith or denomination to another. They cite the classic example of the conversion of Saint Paul in his dramatic change from persecutor of the Church to ardent Christian missioner, which took place during his journey to Damascus (Acts 9:1–19). Conversion certainly implies a radical and fundamental change, but it implies more than a change from one faith or Church to another. For example, it may mean a change from thinking of God as "out there" to thinking of God who is deep within, or from a belief in a God who is in heaven to an awareness of God's presence in our world. It may include a change in our stance in such areas as racism or sexism or toward material possessions, or a change in our behavior toward other people in such matters as forgiveness and reconciliation. All these "conversions" that require a modification of our attitudes or behavior need to be founded on a new and developing understanding of God. Saint Paul's experience on the road to Damascus was not only a call to change from the Jewish to the Christian community. Very much at the center of it was a new awareness of God and how God is incarnate in our world.

The other word to describe this process of growing awareness is *repentance*. We usually think of repentance as meaning to stop sinning, or to break away from bad habits, or to ask forgiveness from God and our neighbor. But when Jesus calls people to repentance, he is asking them to do more than this. He is asking them to change their minds, which is something much more radical. The Greek word that is used in the Scriptures for repentance is *metanoia*. This literally means "change your mind" and is, therefore, much stronger than the usual meaning we give to *repentance*. "Change your mind" is very akin to "conversion." When John the Baptist and Jesus called on their listeners to repent, they were saying, "Change your minds, be converted, change the direction of your lives." People were being asked to make a completely new start, not merely to tinker with a few minor points at the edges.

For a few people, the "conversion" to an awareness of

God's presence can be a sudden and dramatic experience, like that of Saint Paul on the Damascus road. But for the majority of people, the awareness of God's presence in our world and within our hearts comes slowly. It is an experience of gradual growth over a long period. It is something that develops in and through the "joys and hopes, griefs and worries" of our daily existence.

Although this takes a lifetime, there may well come a particular moment when we realize that the presence of God has become very real and certain. There is a tension between this sudden moment of awareness and the gradually emerging consciousness of God's presence, which can be illustrated by a simple reflection on the dawn. The process of the dawn takes place over time, and throughout this it is impossible to tell the difference in the light from one moment to the next. But there still comes a precise point when we know the day has arrived and the night has ended. The commonly used phrase "it suddenly dawned on me…" expresses this well. It implies a gradual process over a time during which change is taking place under the surface and we are not conscious of anything happening, and then a specific moment when everything becomes clear. This is usually how the consciousness of God's presence in our world and the eternal echo in our heart come to our notice.

The God who "visits us like the dawn from on high" is ever present, ever active, in our world and in the daily events of our lives, whether we are conscious of this presence or not. In this sense, God does not "visit us" since that could imply times when God is not with us. But as we become increasingly aware of God abiding in our midst, it will be as though the dawn is coming. The black

and white of the shadows in our hearts will be transformed into color, and the beautiful painting or tapestry
will become more complete; the face of the earth will be
gradually transformed, and the world in all its splendor
will unfold before us.

For Personal Prayer

Before you start to pray, read the notes on page xix about
personal prayer and keep an eye on the suggested pattern
for prayer. The grace you might request in this prayer is
for you to be increasingly aware of God's gentle action in
your life. When you feel ready to move on, read slowly
the following Scripture passage and questions for reflection.

Scripture

The fourth chapter of Saint John's Gospel describes how
a Samaritan woman becomes aware of who Jesus is. This
awareness grows gradually and imperceptibly on the
woman. Like the beginning of the dawn, it is hard to say
at exactly what moment the realization of something extraordinary begins. Jesus gently moves her forward, but
with the certainty and inevitability reminiscent of the
coming of daylight. And as the light grows, so she sees
with greater clarity the events and meaning of her whole
life. If you have a Bible handy, read the whole story from
the fourth chapter of Saint John's Gospel.

Jesus, tired by the journey, sat straight down by the
well....When a Samaritan woman came to draw wa-

ter, Jesus said to her, "Give me a drink." His disciples had gone into the town to buy food.

In the very next verse, Jesus takes the conversation further.

> "If you only knew what God is offering
> and who it is that is saying to you:
> 'Give me a drink,'
> you would have been the one to ask,
> and he would have given you living water."

The woman then asks about this "living water." She is
obviously intrigued by what Jesus is saying. The conversation goes deeper when Jesus reveals that he knows about
her private life.

> The woman put down her water jar and hurried back
> to the town to tell the people, "Come and see a man
> who has told me everything I ever did. I wonder if
> he is the Christ?" This brought people out of the
> town and they started walking towards him....Many
> Samaritans of that town had believed in him on the
> strength of the woman's testimony when she said,
> "He told me all I have ever done," so, when the Sa-
> maritans came up to him, they begged him to stay
> with them. He stayed for two days, and when he
> spoke to them many more came to believe; and they
> said to the woman, "Now we no longer believe be-
> cause of what you told us; we have heard him our-
> selves and we know that he really is the saviour of
> the world."

To Help Your Reflection

- Can I remember times in my life when I have felt a new sense of God's presence? Perhaps I felt God calling me gently to move forward? How do I respond now to this memory?
- Can I remember a particular occasion when something dawned on me or there was a new development in my life? In particular, was there a time when I was struck by a new insight into the ways of God in my life?

At the end of your prayer, spend some time talking to God about what happened. Refer to the grace you asked for and thank God for everything he has done for you. When you are ready, end with an Our Father or Glory Be. Afterward, remember to jot down a few notes for your own benefit later.

In a Listening Group

Once again, refer to the notes on page xxi and keep an eye on the suggested outline of the meeting. In particular, remember the point about these being "listening" groups. The following points are *in addition* to the meeting outline and are to help you in this particular meeting.

Introduce yourselves. If this is the first time you are meeting together, spend a little time getting to know one another. After you have spent a couple of minutes becoming aware of God's presence, go around the group, inviting each person to say their name and something about themselves. The important thing in this, as in the sharing later, is that you simply listen to one another.

Ask for the grace to become more aware of God's gentle action in all your lives.

After everyone has shared and if there is time, you may want to ask if there is anything you can do to help your church or group become more open. How open are we to new ways of understanding something of the presence of God? Do we put up barriers to block new ideas? How well does our church/parish/group cope with change?

2
Our Journey of Faith—
Following the Trail

Our understanding of God and our consequent way of living change and develop throughout life. For this reason, our faith is often likened to a journey. For Christians, this journey begins at our baptism when we set out to follow the way of Christ. The circumstances of our lives may dictate how effectively we manage to follow this path. In this chapter I look at some of the characteristics of the journey of faith.

Chances are that, unless you live in Cumbria, the Scottish Borders, North Yorkshire, or Southern Ireland, you will not have heard of hound trailing. For the uninitiated, let me explain what it is.

Hound trailing is a sport in which dogs race along a previously laid circular trail, usually of six or seven miles. It is not a cruel sport since no animals are hunted or killed. The race over hills and fells is accompanied by all the razzmatazz and side events that add interest and spice to all forms of racing. There are different classes and categories to be entered, trophies to be won, and full on-course betting facilities.

Before the race begins, the trail has to be laid. One of the organizers does this by walking around the course dragging a piece of weighty cloth soaked in a carefully proportioned mixture of aniseed, paraffin, and heavy oil. The course goes high onto the fells and into the dips, hollows, and valleys that are a feature of these upland regions. It goes through mountain streams and becks, over stone walls, and it even crosses roads where, come the race, men with red flags will stop the traffic when the dogs are about to arrive.

Once the trail has been laid, the owners line up with their dogs ready for the start. As the dogs pick up the scent, their eager yelping and barking echoes from the surrounding hills. The final stage of preparation is when someone puts a mark on the neck of each dog to ensure that it cannot be substituted for a fresh dog halfway around the course. When all is ready, a starter waves the flag, and the dogs spring into action, tearing away after the trail, up the fells and into the distance. Occasionally, they can be seen through binoculars high up on the fells, then they are out of sight again.

As an image to help describe a person's religious faith, hound trailing has a lot to commend it. From the first stirring of religious faith, through its development and growth during life, to the final completion in death, a person's awareness of the Divine and the practical response that person makes will change and move on. Consider, for example, the first stirring of religious faith and compare that with the start of a hound trail. Everyone starts a "journey of faith" through life in some way, but for those who are members of a church or faith community, there will be a formal and public ceremony of initiation. For

Christians, this explicit beginning is baptism or "christening." Without excluding the initiation rites of other faith communities, or the beginning of a journey of faith by someone who has no formal attachment to a church or community, I want to use the parallel with hound trailing to refer to baptism, since this is my own tradition and therefore the one with which I am most familiar.

Baptism is the time when Christians are given the "scent" of eternal life, like the hounds being given the "scent" of the trail at the beginning of a race. Perhaps we don't yelp and yowl with quite the same enthusiasm as the hounds, although anyone who has attended the baptism of a baby might be forgiven for thinking so! Nevertheless, the "scent" is given to us, and we set off on a journey that will take us through the ups and downs of life. In our baptism we receive God's life and so become God's children. This is the scent we are given, and it sets us on the journey that leads eventually to eternal life.

The Christian churches sometimes have difficulties with baptism and the other sacraments of initiation, particularly when given to babies or very small children. Should the sacraments be given to those so young that they can know nothing of it? How can the Christian upbringing of the child be guaranteed? How can baptism, and the education that should follow it, be seen as important, when so often adults understand it only as empty ritual? Should baptism be refused when there seems little chance of any follow-up?

In talking of infant baptism, it is principally the parents, and after them the godparents and wider family, who take on the serious responsibility of teaching their child the ways of faith. In the Roman Catholic baptism

service, parents are told that they "are accepting the responsibility of training him/her in the practice of the
faith." To return to the comparison with hound trailing,
just as the dogs have to be trained from puppyhood to
follow the scent of the trail, so, too, from early childhood, we have to be trained by our parents to follow the
ways of God. If there is no training by parents, the "scent"
of faith has little chance of survival, and there is, therefore, little point in bringing a child for baptism in these
circumstances. Hounds would soon lose interest if they
followed trails that led nowhere!

So much for the start of the hound trail. What happens
next? The dogs, well-trained, at the peak of fitness, eager
and alert, set off in pursuit of the trail. The pungent mixture of aniseed, paraffin, and heavy oil leads off into the
distance. Where their journey will take them neither they
nor their owners know. Certainly the trail will wind its way
"over the hills and far away." It will not all be easy going,
and it will test the dogs and bring out the best in them.

Our journey through life, too, will take us into all sorts
of strange places. There will be hills with steep inclines
and rough patches where the going gets tough and we
think we will never make it. There will also be gentle
downhill slopes where our feet feel carefree and we make
progress quickly. Our trail will take us through beautiful
places and into dark and desolate valleys. At the outset
we cannot imagine where the trail may lead. And when
we look back on our past journey, we marvel at what we
have been through and how we have coped and we think,
"I would never have imagined that my life would have
followed that path."

When we think back over our lives and call to mind the

times when we were aware of the presence of God in certain events, we are remembering and getting in touch with our journey of faith. In the big events of our lives—growing up, falling in love, marriage, childbirth, bereavement, sickness—God has always been with us, whether we have been aware of his presence or not. In the smaller events, too, the material world of our everyday lives touches and overlaps with the spiritual world, the eternal, the "other." Our faith history is simply the story of the intertwining of these two worlds in the lives of each of us.

Of course, that is not the full story, either for the hounds or for us! At the beginning of the race, the hounds start off full of eagerness, closely following the trail with every sinew and every ounce of strength. But as the race goes on, they can often lose their way. They may lose the scent for a time and wander aimlessly until they manage to find it again. Occasionally, they lose their way completely, and their owners have to go off into the hills to find them and bring them home, bedraggled, tired, and downhearted. On our journey of faith we, too, sometimes lose the scent. We forget the call of our baptism and the eternal life for which we are destined. We wander off on our own, perhaps thinking we can find a better way than the trail laid for us. We may find our way back eventually, but sometimes we can lose the trail more permanently. In these times when we are hopelessly lost, God comes to search for us, eagerly wanting our return. The good owner of the hound, like the good shepherd, will search high and low, late into the evening, until finding the one that was lost. And in spite of feeling disappointment at not winning the race, the good owner will comfort the dog, not cajole and admonish it.

It is important to be in touch with our own personal faith history if we are to develop our awareness of God further. This is something that is acknowledged in every area of spirituality. For example, in the great Christian annual retreat that we call Lent, the readings that are used in church services by all denominations invite us to look into our faith. When adults approach the Christian community, asking to know more, an important part of their initiation is being in touch with their own personal faith journey so far. By recognizing the ways of God in the past, we become more alert to God's action in the present, and we also acquire hope and trust for the future. "If God has done all this for me," we can say, "then surely God will continue to look after me, whatever comes?" Just as hounds learn by experience to trust and follow their owners, so we learn by experience, and by reflection on that experience, to trust more deeply in God.

And so, after a long hard race, the hounds reach the homestretch. They are urged on by their owners and backers, and called forward to the prize of some tasty tidbits after a job well done, a race well run. Some will be lagging behind, perhaps limping from a minor injury, or tired and weary because it was all too much for them. But they are all welcomed and rewarded because, well, at least they have tried. I feel sure that if hound trailing had existed at the time of Jesus, he would have used it in a parable! Perhaps Saint Paul came closest to it when he wrote about "racing for the finish, running the course, straining for the prize which is waiting for us."

At the end of our faith journey on earth there is the "prize" awaiting us—a life of eternal happiness. Whether we have run a straight clean race or got into all sorts of trouble on the way, we are still eagerly awaited at the finish. In the end, it matters little where our journey has taken us. We may have wandered off the main trail, got bogged down in murky places, even gone in completely the wrong direction. God will still be impatiently waiting for us. Whether we romp home at the head of the field or limp in wounded and tired, the important thing is that we get there. And when we do, no matter what has happened in the meantime, we can be assured that we will be welcomed home with open arms.

For Personal Prayer

Until you are used to the suggested pattern of prayer, you may need to refer again to the outline given on page xix. The grace you might ask for in this chapter is the gift of being able to discover the path you have followed in your journey of faith so far, and to appreciate God's action in your past life.

Scripture

When you are ready, slowly read the following Scripture passage. This is the story of the call of the first disciples in Saint John's Gospel (1:35–51). As we read the story, we hear of the "scent" being given to the disciples, of their response, and of how they passed it on to others. After you have read the story, notice any phrases or words that stand out for you.

John stared hard at Jesus and said, "Look, there is the lamb of God." Hearing this, the two disciples

followed Jesus. Jesus turned round, saw them following and said, "What do you want?" They an-
swered, "Rabbi,"—which means Teacher—"where
do you live?" "Come and see" he replied; so they
went and saw where he lived, and stayed with him
the rest of that day....

Early next morning, Andrew met his brother
[Simon Peter] and said to him, "We have found the
Messiah"—which means the Christ—and he took
Simon to Jesus....

The pattern is repeated the next day when Jesus invites
Philip to follow him and Philip in turn goes to tell
Nathaniel who, although skeptical at first, accepts Philip's
invitation to "come and see." Nathaniel has a change of
heart through conversation with Jesus, who promises he
"will see greater things than that."

To Help Your Reflection

In the light of this gospel, I spend some time looking back
over my life with Jesus. I try to recognize and acknowledge the moments when God has touched my life. In particular, I might focus on some of the following points:

- When did I first become aware of God? What brought
  about this awareness? How did I feel about it then and
  how do I feel about it now? Has this awareness of God's
  presence deepened as time has gone on?
- In the gospel passage, the invitation to "come and see"
  is repeated and is impelling. In what circumstances in
  my past have I heard this same invitation being ad-

dressed to me? How did I respond then? Do I hear the invitation now? If so, how do I respond? If not, do I want to hear it or would I rather it went away?

- Their acceptance of the invitation was to lead the disciples into places they could never have imagined. What have been the unexpected things of my life? Am I happy with the way my faith journey has progressed? What have been the good aspects and what have been the less good aspects of my faith journey?

In a Listening Group

Ask for the grace to become more aware of God's call and loving support in all your lives. As well as sharing what happened in your prayer time, you might like to share some of the significant events in your own faith journey. Don't feel you have to share anything you don't want to. Remember, it is important to listen to the stories of others and so make sure to allow everyone an equal chance to tell their stories. Really listen to their stories, don't just pretend to do so.

After everyone has shared and if there is time, you may want to deepen the reflection by a short discussion on the following points:

- Notice that having been called himself, Philip went to tell Nathaniel. How easy do I find it to tell others about my faith and about my relationship with God? Can I share a time when I was asked for my experience?
- If I am involved in the Christian education of others, particularly as a parent or a godparent, how seriously do I take these responsibilities?

3
The Church—
Our Fellow Travelers

I t goes without saying that our journey of faith through life is not undertaken in isolation. We are in the company of others from whom we can learn much and who help us on our way. In this chapter, I look at what it means to be part of a "pilgrim people" and explore the effects of companionship on our journey.

From the very earliest times and throughout the history of the Church, pilgrimages have been a major part of the Christian landscape. Over the centuries, major routes of pilgrimage developed—to the Holy Land, to Santiago de Compostello, to Rome, and to Canterbury. Pilgrims embarked on their once-in-a-lifetime journey not knowing what awaited them, how long they would be away, or, indeed, whether they would ever return. Their goodbyes to family and friends before departure would have had an air of finality: the end of a past life and the start of something completely new. Their journey into the unknown was one of adventure, in which they sought the answer to life's mysteries and searched for fulfillment and happiness. Whether they went to atone for some serious misdemeanor or simply out of devotion, their quest was brave and courageous.

Look through religious newspapers and periodicals today and you will find countless advertisements for pilgrimages. To the ancient destinations have been added more recent shrines such as Lourdes, Fátima, and Medjugorje. However, modern travel has taken away the element of uncertainty. Pilgrims no longer embark on a journey into the unknown; full-color brochures make sure of that. And any travel agent who did not guarantee a safe return home would be struck off the list! In fact, there may be little nowadays to distinguish a package pilgrimage from a package holiday, except the fact that prayer and worship will be included, and the destinations will have religious connections. While some may lament the passing of harsher former pilgrimages, the greater safety and availability today must be welcomed.

It is quite likely that most people reading this have, at some time or other, been on a pilgrimage. It may have been a fortnight in the Holy Land or in Rome, or a day trip to the local Marian shrine. What have our pilgrimages been like? Who have our fellow pilgrims been? What did we learn from the experience? There are many parallels between our pilgrimages to shrines and holy places and our journey of faith through life.

It is quite likely that we have memories of some of the people who were on the pilgrimage with us. A motley crew, no doubt! We may remember the "pray-ers," who offered multiple decades of the rosary; the "curious," who explored every corner of every shrine; and the "carers," for whom the pilgrimage was about looking after sick and elderly fellow pilgrims. There may even have been some who were, literally, "only here for the beer" and for whom the pilgrimage was the social event of the year. We may recall that on our pilgrimage there was the usual mixture of "old stagers," who regaled the company with exaggerated stories of pilgrimages past, and bewildered "first timers," who wondered what they had let themselves in for. There were those who wanted to "do" as much as possible, rushing everywhere so as not to waste a single moment; and others who tried to slow things down to match their own pace. There were happy people, for whom everything was wonderful; and the grumblers, who found fault everywhere. Some made lasting friendships with their fellow pilgrims; others found someone whom they could not tolerate. Yes, it takes all types of people to make up a pilgrimage.

In the Book of Exodus, the second book of the Bible, we are told the epic tale of the pilgrimage, or journey, of Moses and the people of Israel. Here we read the story of the forming of a nation and, more important, of the early days of a people who would be God's people. We read of the trials and tribulations they went through during forty years in the desert. Reading between the lines, we know they were not a neat and orderly group of people but something more akin to the disparate and ragged group that makes up any pilgrimage. Maps of the probable route of this emerging people show how they constantly wandered backward and forward. Splinter groups went off in different directions. Sometimes they found their way back, sometimes they became completely lost. On some occasions, they stayed in one place for many months or even years, at other times they moved swiftly on. This pilgrim people, God's Chosen People, was little more than a ragged and chaotic group of nomads wandering through the desert.

The Exodus story is a template for the journeys of all faith communities and for all people as they struggle with the fundamental questions of life and death in the company of others. Once again I shall use this template, and the idea of pilgrimages in general, to make some observations from my own church background. Similar ideas can be applied to situations outside the Christian context.

The Christian churches have been described as the people of God on pilgrimage, and our reflection on pilgrimages and the Exodus story can help to illustrate some of the implications of this. Like pilgrims, those who make up the Church are diverse and, at times, irregular. There are many individual differences between members. There are those who want to go faster and urge the whole group to keep up; others who drag their feet and hold everyone back. Many wander off on their own ways, sometimes finding their way back, sometimes getting totally lost.

This is not a popular image of any of the churches. Outsiders taking a cursory glance at the churches, with ideas gleaned from the media and from a few personal acquaintances, expect everyone who belongs to a church to believe and do exactly the same things. If they were to describe the Church, they might say that it was like an army marching in formation. They envisage everyone wearing the same uniform, all in step, unthinking and conformist, eyes straight ahead, oblivious to what is going on around them. When a church or parish conforms to this image, it is deemed to be "a good thing"; when it shows diversity and uncertainty, it is universally condemned.

The reality of any of the churches, as those who are members will be only too aware, is much closer to that of the ragged pilgrim people than to that of an army marching in formation. This latter image, while it might be popular, causes problems for non-Christians who, even if they wanted to, think they would never be worthy enough or intelligent enough to have enough willpower to be part of the Church. To become a member, they think, one has to be very holy, able to keep all the rules, charitable, good living, prayerful. No wonder there are few people knocking on our doors, clamoring to join us! Somehow, we need to be seen as communities that will welcome all sorts of folks and who will not demand extraordinary perfection and conformity. In other words, the churches need to be seen as pilgrim peoples.

Pilgrims have to learn to be tolerant of their fellow travelers. People of different backgrounds and cultures, with disparate views and diverse ways of acting, have to get on together. There must be understanding and mutual acceptance, even when disagreement remains. There is no place in a pilgrim people for prejudice against a group that is unconventional, no place for bigotry of any kind. Within the churches as a whole and within each diocese, parish, and organization, everyone needs to ask themselves how understanding and welcoming they are to others. In some communities, for example, there may be prejudice between different ethnic groups or against people of other races, women, homosexuals, or poor people. Accepting others as part of the same pilgrim people does not mean agreeing with them about everything, nor does it mean having to like everyone. But the fact that we are all on the same pilgrimage together means that we are brothers and sisters, fellow travelers on the same journey. Tolerance, understanding, and full acceptance of everyone are the hallmarks of a truly pilgrim people.

The churches must not shirk from being seen to be on the side of the poorest, the disadvantaged, the oppressed. On any pilgrimage, people need others to help them along. In particular, sick, elderly, and disabled people, and those who are weakest, need the encouragement, care, and support of others. Of their very nature, pilgrimages work only when everyone pulls together so that the strong help the weak, the fit carry the disabled, the young care for the old. A key characteristic of the Church should be its care for the weakest. The fact that this is not generally seen to be so probably indicates that it is not as true as it should be, or as we within the churches persuade ourselves that it is.

So much for the motley crew that makes up our pilgrim people. What other lessons can we learn from the idea of pilgrimage? Think back for a moment to those medieval pilgrimages in far distant lands. What a spirit of adventure must have been present! Imagine what a tremendous decision it must have been to set out on such a journey and how much preparation, spiritually and materially, there must have been. And what would it have been like at the time of leaving, saying a tearful goodbye to family and friends, setting off on foot into the unknown—with the distinct possibility of never returning?

Our pilgrimage of faith through life is also one of adventure. There is so much to explore in our relationship with God, so much to find out, so much to investigate. To fully experience faith, it is necessary to make a decision that we want to go forward into the unknown. If we are timid or overly cautious, if we hold back, afraid of what may happen next, we will never know the fullness of the gift that is faith. It is not easy to take any step in the dark, and many Christians never find the courage fully to do this. It is human nature to want to look for the safe path, to cling to the familiar, to follow tried and tested ways. The pity is that the lives of so many become impoverished by this timidity. Fullness of life, the life Jesus offers to all his followers, will be possible only when we have, like the early pilgrims, a sense of adventure in our quest for God and the eternal.

There is one final and very important lesson from our reflection on pilgrimages. In ancient times pilgrims went on foot. The less baggage they carried, the easier and faster their journey became. Even with modern transport, a pilgrim today who turns up with too much luggage can be a burden on the whole party. And airlines impose heavy fines on those who carry so much luggage that they exceed the weight limit.

Thinking of ourselves as part of a pilgrim people should lead us to ask some searching questions about the baggage we each try to carry. This excess baggage can come from our upbringing or from circumstances in our lives. It may be emotional or have to do with our faith and belief. It may include prejudices of one sort or another, fears and anxiety, an unwillingness to "let go," or some idea we have picked up somewhere that we regard as almost sacred. Simply admitting that we have too much baggage may be the first step toward traveling more lightly and thus toward greater freedom. Finding what our excess baggage is will require prayer and discussion with another trusted person, such as a spiritual director or close friend. We will also need an openness to God's work in our lives, a humility that accepts our need of God, and a trust that God will look after us totally. Having discovered what excess baggage we carry, the real challenge is in trying to discard some of it. This is where our pilgrimage really begins, for we will need all the courage God can give us as we embark on our adventure.

For Personal Prayer

Spend a moment or two thinking about the chapter, then notice if there is a grace that emerges for you. Otherwise, choose a grace from the following:

- to be a better member of a "pilgrim people";
- to be more tolerant and understanding of other people in the Church;
- to be able to see what "excess baggage" I am carrying and what can be discarded.

Scripture

The parable of the Good Shepherd in Saint John's Gospel (10:1–16) is an appropriate one for this theme of pilgrimage. In the culture of the time, and still today in parts of the Middle East, shepherds were people who lived with their flocks day and night. They traveled with them, protected them, and knew them. During the day, the flocks would wander freely far and wide, guided by the shepherd who knew where the best grazing was likely to be.

When you feel ready, read these phrases from the parable and stay with anything that appeals to you.

"I am the gate of the sheepfold....
Anyone who enters through me will be safe:
he will go freely in and out
and be sure of finding pasture....
I have come
so that they may have life
and have it to the full.
I am the good shepherd:
the good shepherd is one who lays down his life for
his sheep....
I know my own
and my own know me."

To Help Your Reflection

- How do I feel about the parable of the Good Shepherd? Do I feel as if Christ is my Good Shepherd, taking care of me? You may want to spend some time talking to him about this.
- Thinking about herds of sheep and groups of pilgrims, how do I feel about being part of a ragged, wandering bunch of people? Am I comfortable with this? Would I prefer a group that is all in step? In general, do I prefer things to be black and white or can I cope with "gray" areas?
- How do I get on with my fellow pilgrims? Are there any particular individuals or groups of people whom I find it difficult to tolerate? Can I talk to the Good Shepherd about this?
- Does my following of Christ ever feel like an exciting adventure? Or is it just boring? Am I afraid to step out into the unknown? How do I cope with uncertainty?

- What "excess baggage" do I carry? Where did it come from? How does it feel to consider getting rid of some of it? Do I want to try to lighten the load in order to travel more easily on my journey of faith?

In a Listening Group

You might want to ask each person in turn simply to mention the grace they were praying for during the week. Or you may prefer to ask for the grace to become free of the baggage that each one of us carries with us.

As well as sharing what happened in your prayer time, you could also say how you feel about the church, parish, or group to which you belong. Remember to listen to everyone, even when they may say critical things. You might also include any feelings and thoughts you have about the "excess baggage" that you as a church, parish, or group may have.

To deepen the reflection, after everyone has shared and if there is time, you may want to open out into discussion again and ask yourselves how, as a parish or group, can we begin to travel more lightly?

4
Witness and Evangelization

In this chapter, I show how the light that Christ brings is not just for our own benefit but for others', and I examine what role each Christian has in letting this light illuminate the world.

Lighthouses are familiar sights around the coasts of Britain. In prominent positions on headlands and estuaries, on rocky outcrops and small offshore islands, they are a commonplace feature of the coastal landscape. With the coming of modern electronic guidance systems, most are not used nowadays, but over the centuries lighthouses have guided ships in safety through fair conditions and foul.

I remember a lighthouse keeper on a remote offshore island once showing me around his domain. The lighthouse was situated high on the cliff top. We entered through a small door set into the base of the tower and climbed a cramped spiral staircase up the ever-narrowing central core. Knowing that the light shone many miles out to sea, I had fully expected to find an enormous light bulb, much bigger than our normal domestic bulbs. Instead, something totally unexpected greeted me.

At the very center of the lighthouse was nothing more than a tiny gaslight. It was daytime, and when the lighthouse keeper lit the gas, it hardly gave out any light at all. Although it was only inches from our faces, the light was barely visible. But surrounding this pinpoint of light were mirrors and prisms and reflectors and a multitude of magnifying lenses. The lighthouse keeper explained it to me like this: "The gaslight," he said, "hardly looks anything in itself and has very little power on its own. But its light shines out many miles in different directions. The mirrors and reflectors magnify the light and transmit it far and wide." My visit to the lighthouse took place several years ago, and I may not have remembered all the technical details. But the image of the tiny light shining out so powerfully through the magnifying lenses has etched itself on my memory.

People of different faiths have their own particular ways of describing God's presence and action in the world, and their own traditions of prayer and worship. For Christians, the focus of prayer and worship is Jesus Christ because in him is the fullest revelation of God. Because Christ is considered to be the light of the world, I want to use the image of the lighthouse to describe something of God's ways and of the response that the followers of Christ are called to give.

Christians believe that two thousand years ago a tiny light shone for a few years in a remote and primitive part of the world called Palestine. This light was the life and work of Jesus Christ. The light was minuscule in comparison with the whole of world history. Its immediate and direct influence was on very few people in a small part of the world. Like the gaslight at the heart of the lighthouse, the light of Christ hardly seemed big enough to reach very far or to penetrate the darkness.

But in spite of its limitations of time and space, the life of Christ brought the promise of a new quality of life, freedom, and happiness. The revelation about God that Christ brought was a light that shone in the midst of darkness, sin, and death. At first, of course, it could only bring this revelation about the involvement of God in our lives to a few hundred people in that remote and relatively insignificant part of the world. But later it would spread far beyond those narrow confines to embrace the whole world for all time.

Who could ever have guessed that it would become such a powerful light shining into every part of the world, in every age? Who could have predicted that it would penetrate some of the darkest corners of human life? And who, among the people living at the time of Christ, could ever have known that the insight into the life of God that Christ gave would be so far-reaching? For all this to happen, certain outside agents were necessary. Just as the light at the center of the lighthouse had to be surrounded by some means of magnification in order to reach far out, so too the light of Christ has to be transmitted and reflected and magnified.

The followers of Christ from the earliest times have been the mirrors and reflectors and magnifying lenses that have transmitted his light to the world. In as much as each individual Christian and the whole Church have been faithful to this, so the light of Christ has shone clearly. Where Christians, individually and as a community, have failed to let the light of Christ through, there darkness has prevailed.

There has been much talk recently in the Christian churches about evangelism and evangelization, particularly in the context of the "Decade of Evangelization/ Evangelism." This has left many Christians and local communities feeling at a loss as to what to do about it. We have all asked questions such as *What do these things mean?* And, more particularly, *What has to be done? What is meant by "witnessing" to Christ, and what is the proper way to give good example?* Perhaps the best answer to these questions is to say that evangelization and evangelism simply mean that we must be the reflectors, mirrors, and lenses through which the light of Christ can shine. We do so in the knowledge that we are not "bringing" Christ to the world. We cannot do that because he is already here, present in all things. What we are doing is letting the light of Christ illuminate the darkness so that others can come to know that presence too.

The quality we need to let the light of Christ shine through us is transparency. The task of each one of us, a task that is an easy yoke and a light burden, is to become so transparent that the light of Christ shines clearly through us to reach the rest of the world. By showing in our everyday lives honesty, integrity, good living, joy, and kindness, we are being true to our calling as followers of Christ. When any individual Christian lives a good life, or when a Christian community gives a healthy and life-giving witness, it is not their own goodness or perfection that they are proclaiming, it is not their own light that is shining. True witness means the type of self-forgetfulness that makes us so transparent that the light that is Christ's life shines clearly through us to others.

As in so many things in the spiritual life, it is not so much the striving to do something or to overcome some obstacle that is important. Rather, the mark of a true fol-

lower of Christ is the ability to let Christ take over. Being
a witness to the gospel is not about engaging in frenzied
activity or spending lots of time doing something extraordinary. It is in being, not doing; in letting God increase
and ourselves decrease. When the awareness of God in
us and around us has dawned on us, the light from this
insight will automatically radiate outward from us. If we
are to help others grow in their awareness of God's presence and action in the world, it is what we are, not what
we do, that will count.

If we think about it, most of us know people who have
this quality of transparency. They are often the little
people, the poor in spirit, those who feel they can't cope
with a problem or with life itself. In fact, the transparent
people are the ones who were described by Jesus in those
few verses of the gospel that we call the Beatitudes (at the
beginning of chapter 5 of Saint Matthew's Gospel). Jesus
pointed out for special mention the merciful, those who
mourn, peacemakers, those who hunger and thirst for
what is right, and so on. There is a quality about these
people that can only be described as transparent. They
have nothing to boast about in themselves, and, therefore,
they turn in complete trust to God. It has been through
people such as these throughout the ages that Christ has
chosen to let his light shine. Just as glass that is clear and
clean lets the full brightness of the light shine through, so
Christians must be transparent and clear, to let the brightness and beauty of Christ's light into the world.

Let us return to our lighthouse. On the side facing out
to sea, the glass was clear and transparent to allow through
the maximum amount of light. But on the landward side,
the glass was completely darkened and blocked off so

that no light at all could get through. Where Christians are transparent, like those described in the Beatitudes, the light of Christ will go out far and wide, clear like crystal. But there are times when the followers of Christ stand in the way of the light and block the message completely.

This blocking of Christ's light can come about because someone is trying to bolster up a particular political viewpoint or to give added weight to their own personal opinion. Almost always the problem is rooted in an abuse of power. Whenever there is self-seeking or pride, vested interests or pressure groups, power and domination, then the light of Christ is diminished or distorted. For there is no place in the Christian life for greed, selfishness, or self seeking of any sort. There is no room for bigotry or narrow-mindedness or power games. These are the things that, at worst, block the light totally or, at best, give a distorted light, a dim light, a flickering light.

I have one final reflection about the lighthouse to conclude this chapter. One quarter of the glass was tinted red, clearly warning of the danger of hidden rocks. This colored light reminded me of the rainbow, in which can be seen the many different colors that blend together and combine to give pure white light. Each color is a necessary part of the whole picture, each must be present, and all must be in harmony.

The light of Christ shines through Christians in different ways. For example, some give a prophetic message by involvement in justice and peace issues; others care for those in need; others again are teachers, preachers, or administrators. And God works through individuals in many other ways, too varied to single out here. These different "lights" are like the different colors of the rainbow: they all have their place in making up the one, clear light of Christ. If any "color" starts thinking of itself as the only one and tries to make everyone else do the same, then the light becomes distorted. Recognizing, acknowledging, and affirming the gifts and contributions of others lead to the true and clear light of Christ shining out to illuminate the whole world.

This is what we call the Church, and it is beautifully described as follows:

As Christ's Church we are called into being
to reflect his light.
The Church has no light except the light
of Jesus Christ;
it has no truth except him;
it has no love to give,
no forgiveness,
no compassion
except that of Jesus Christ.
The Church is indeed a mirror of Christ,
reflecting in the world the light of him
who is "the glorious splendour of the Father."
When, as the Church, we are focused on Christ,
then we shine with his light;
when the Church is turned in on itself,
then it is as dark as the fading moon,
no more than a sliver of light in the night sky.
Our task is none other than that of reflecting the
light of Christ to our whole world, to our society.

(These words come from a reflection written by the Roman Catholic bishops of England and Wales following a week of study in September 1993.)

For Personal Prayer

As before, start by sitting quietly for a minute or two. The grace you might ask for is the gift of knowing that Christ's light shines through you, or the grace to be as transparent as possible.

Scripture

When you feel ready, slowly read the following Scripture passage. This is the prologue of Saint John's Gospel (1:1–18) and is a wonderful meditation on Christ, the light of the world, and on our responsibility to let that light shine through us. After you have read it, stay with any words or phrases that seem to stand out for you.

> In the beginning was the Word,
> the Word was with God
> and the Word was God....
> All that came to be had life in him
> and that life was the light of men,
> a light that shines in the dark,
> a light that darkness could not overpower.

The next paragraph refers to John the Baptist who was preparing the way for Jesus.

A man came, sent by God.
His name was John.
He came as a witness,
as a witness to speak for the light,
so that everyone might believe through him.
He was not the light,
only a witness to speak for the light.

To Help Your Reflection

- Like John the Baptist, I am called to be someone who lets Christ shine to the world. Is that a new idea for me? What does it feel like? Do I sometimes get in the way of Christ's light?
- Can I think of someone I know or knew who impressed me by their life or their words? (Perhaps this may be a teacher, a parent, a neighbor, or a friend.) Could I recognize Christ in what they said or did? How did they help me to grow and develop?
- Can I remember a time when I tried to witness to Christ or a time when I made an effort to be Christlike in something I said or did? Why did I try? What importance do I place on giving a good example? Does this link up in any way for me with "evangelization" or "evangelism"?
- I think about my local church or group of churches. How do we bear witness to the gospel? Do people recognize the light of Christ shining through our communities?

In a Listening Group

When you are ready to start, light the candle, which is a particularly appropriate symbol for this chapter. Begin by asking for the grace to listen well to one another. Follow this with five minutes of silence, recalling your personal prayer. You might include in your sharing any thoughts you have about the church, parish, or group to which you belong and reflect on how, as a community, you bear witness to the gospel? Do people recognize the light of Christ shining through you? To deepen your reflection, you might like to discuss what your local community needs to do to reflect the light in a clearer way.

5
Prayer—
Tuning In to God

God is everywhere, in our world and in our hearts. This presence is like the multitude of radio waves that crowd our skies even though we cannot see them. In this chapter, I want to explore how we tune in to this presence and so become more deeply conscious of the mystery of God.

Some people will remember that, in the days before television, many houses had a large and cumbersome wireless set. Why they were called "wireless" I'm not sure because the insides were full of wires! One of my early memories is of playing with our old-fashioned wireless set at home when I was quite small. I remember clearly that it had long-wave, medium-wave, and three short-wave bands.

To me, as a small boy, the long-wave was always relatively boring. There was something called "The Home Service" (now the more prosaic Radio 4), three or four French stations, and not much else. The medium-wave band promised richer pickings. As well as the Light Programme, now Radio 2, and the Third Programme,

Radio 3, there were other sounds and signals that I could understand because they were in English: Radio Eirean, the Voice of America, and Radio Luxembourg spring to mind. There were also the illegal pirate stations beginning with Radio Caroline moored off the Isle of Man and then extending to others whose names I can't now recall. These were always full of adventure, intrigue, and mystery. Listening to them felt very daring. But it wasn't tuning to any of these stations that attracted me most, but going slowly through the dial picking up snatches of the many and various sounds and messages from faraway places. And it was on the shortwave bands that the greatest source of interest lay. I would spend hours in the evening, driving my mother and father mad, listening for faint signals in languages I didn't understand or in Morse code or in some other coded signal. When I found something that I thought might be interesting, I would wait for the turn of the hour to see if I could make out which radio station it was and where it was broadcasting from. I even learned, badly, how to decipher Morse code and occasionally would pick up a signal in which the Morse was slow enough for me to recognize a few letters.

Thinking about the myriad radio signals that, although invisible and unnoticed, crowd our skies can lead us to reflect on the nature of God's presence everywhere and in all things. At the same time, going through the dial on a wireless set, trying to pick up signals and messages, can help us to understand something about the way this omnipresent God communicates with us. It can also point the way to valuable insights about how we receive the signals.

Everything about us reflects something of God, and as we go about our daily lives we can become more sensitive to this. We live in a world that is God's playground, which he sees as being "very good," where his Son was born and lived, where his Spirit is present and active. God communicates something of his mystery to us through this world. God is to be found in all things, not just in the beauties of the natural world but also in the world created by people, in the towns and cities and in society generally. When we tune in to all this, we can hear God's word—a Word that became incarnate and that is very close to us. Often it is easier to see the bad things about our world and to stand back and criticize. And it is certainly true that there is no shortage of bad news. Stories of sin and evil abound, and human failing and weakness may seem to overwhelm everything good. But tuning in to the reality around us also means being sensitive to the joys and hopes, as well as the griefs and sorrows of our neighbors and colleagues. Strange as it may appear, we can actually discover God in the worlds of politics, business, entertainment, commerce, and so on.

Some of the messages in the world surrounding us can clearly raise our thoughts to God. We might remember times we have been overwhelmed by the beauty of nature, an act of kindness or courage, a story of heroism, or an example of integrity. God can be discerned in the bright skies that promise future happiness, or in birdsong on a spring day, or in love freely given and received. These are the messages that are clear and coherent, in a language we can understand and in a logical format that makes sense. They are like the strong, clear signals we pick up on the wireless dial. It is easy to see how God is revealed in them.

But many of the messages we receive are confused and difficult to understand. We hear of a tragedy in which, perhaps, children have been killed or abused, and we ask why. We receive some bad personal news and wonder if we'll be able to cope. We learn that people we have respected have not lived up to their promises. We hear of pain and sorrow, of boredom and despair, of confusion and evil. And God does not seem to be in these more difficult situations. These are coded messages, like the messages in Morse code, which need deciphering before we can understand them. At first it seems impossible to make sense of them, and even after a struggle we often fail to understand how God can be in them or what they can reveal of the mystery of the Divine. Yet God communicates with us through these coded, difficult bulletins as well as through the messages that are clear and obvious.

Just as the air is full of radio signals in every possible format and language, so God's presence is all around us and within us. All we have to do is tune in! But if God is so clearly in all things, why do we find it so difficult to listen to and to be conscious of God's presence? Sometimes people say, "Why is it that whenever I pray to God, all that seems to come back is a resounding silence? Why doesn't God answer my prayer? Why doesn't God give me guidance and help and consolation?" Sometimes these doubts come in a slightly different form. We say to God, "I've always tried to live a good life, to keep the commandments, to go to church, to say my prayers, why don't you reward me? Why don't I feel you near to me?" And then we end up feeling frustrated and powerless in the face of a resounding silence from the Almighty. These questions and difficulties are pondered by Christians and by many other people who are trying to live a good life and grow toward God. I want to mention briefly a few of the reasons for these difficulties and then offer some positive suggestions as to how we might tune in to God more effectively.

In the first place, prayer can be difficult because too often we are the ones who do all the talking. Prayer becomes a monologue in which we spend our time giving God all the details of our situation and pleading with many words. If we are the ones doing all the talking, how can there be any space for God to speak to us? We would find it difficult to listen to a radio program if we were talking at the same time. If God is to "get a word in edgewise," then we need to stop talking and learn how to listen.

Second, we frequently use words about prayer such as "God speaking to us," "hearing God's word," "listening to what God has to say to us." All these phrases speak of verbal communication, and our expectations are that there will be a verbal message from God. So we listen for voices or we look at written words and expect God to speak to us in those verbal ways. While many forms of prayer are verbal, we need to recognize the nonverbal communication too. God can be revealed through our feelings, instinct, and intuition. These are the coded messages that, like Morse code or even music on our radios, need to be deciphered but that are nonetheless real and important.

Third, we sometimes look for God in the wrong place, and God's presence is unexpected. Rather like the prophet Elijah (in 1 Kings 19:9–13), who waited at the door of his cave for God to pass by. A storm came, an earthquake, and a mighty wind, and we can imagine Elijah thinking that God must be in these great meteorological events and being quite disappointed when God wasn't. But it was in the gentle breeze, the most unlikely of the circumstances, that God chose to become manifest. Sometimes, religious teaching can overemphasize the transcendence of God. This leads to the impression that God is very distant, "in the heavens," and way beyond our reach. If we only listen for a distant God, we are likely to be disappointed. Distant signals on our radio are the weakest! God is also revealed close to us, in the world all around us and through the people and events that are nearest. It is from here that the strongest signals will come.

For all these reasons, everyone finds prayer difficult at times. Even though God is all about us and within us, tuning in to God's presence may elude us. So what do we need to do to begin to tune in? How are we best able to receive God's communication with us? In other chapters in this book I explore some ways of becoming more conscious of God's presence. Here I want to point out one or two aspects of our prayer that become clearer through comparison with tuning in to a radio station.

Most important of all is the desire to be in touch with God who is near, just as we must want to listen to the radio if we are to go to the trouble of tuning in. It really is as simple as that. Without that basic desire nothing will ever happen. Picking out God's presence from the cacophony of sounds that surround us is not easy. But it becomes impossible if we are halfhearted or if we lack the enthusiasm to make much effort. Given that basic desire, God can then take over, and we will be surprised how often and in how many different ways God communicates with us.

Next there are those attitudes to prayer that I have already mentioned above. Namely, that we do not do all the talking but spend some time listening too; that we are aware of our feelings, instincts, or intuition and understand these as equally important ways of "hearing" God's revelation for us; and that we are willing to discern God's presence and message very close to us and within our hearts. In many ways, these basic attitudes to prayer are more important than lengthy set formulas or many of the other things often associated with prayer. In a sense, they are like turning the radio on in the first place. If we have failed to do that, no amount of fiddling with the controls will have any effect!

Given these basic attitudes, our prayer may have some surprising results. Just as tuning in to different stations on the radio broadens our horizons and puts us instantly in touch with places we will never otherwise visit, so being open to God's message for us opens the way to a whole new world. It is impossible to anticipate what God wants for each of us, but God will open up new avenues, some of which we may never have dreamed existed. That is the adventure that is before us.

For Personal Prayer

The grace you might like to ask for in this prayer time is to be ready to tune in to God's word for you and the courage to be open to accepting that word.

Scripture

The gospel stories about the first Easter Sunday morning tell of the disciples' looking for Jesus in the wrong place. They look in the tomb to find him; they should be looking elsewhere. An openness to searching in new places rather than in the expected ones is what is called for. One of the most remarkable stories is that of Mary of Magdala as told in Saint John's Gospel (20:11–18). Read this story slowly and note any words or ideas that stand out for you.

Meanwhile Mary stayed outside near the tomb, weeping. Then, still weeping, she stooped to look inside, and saw two angels in white sitting where the body of Jesus had been, one at the head, the other at the feet. They said, "Woman, why are you weeping?" "They have taken my Lord away" she replied "and I don't know where they have put him." As she said this she turned round and saw Jesus standing there, though she did not recognize him. Jesus said, "Woman, why are you weeping? Who are you looking for?" Supposing him to be the gardener, she said, "Sir, if you have taken him away, tell me where you have put him, and I will go and remove him." Jesus said, "Mary!" She knew him then and said to him in Hebrew, "Rabbuni!"—which means Master. Jesus said to her, "Do not cling to me, because I have not yet ascended to the Father. But go and find the brothers and tell them. I am ascending to my Father and your Father, to my God and your God." So Mary of Magdala went and told the disciples that she had seen the Lord and that he had said these things to her.

To Help Your Reflection

- I try to imagine myself in the place of Mary in this scene. How do I feel before I recognize Jesus, and how do I feel afterward?
- I think back over my life. When did God seem absent, and when did I recognize God's presence, often in the unexpected? How did I cope with these different situations?
- Am I more comfortable with a God who is very distant "in the heavens," or with a God who is close to me? How easy do I find it to tune in to a God who is in the world around me? What have I discovered of God's presence when I have reflected on the events and people of my life?

In a Listening Group

Refer again to the pattern for a listening group on page xxii. The grace you might ask for is to be able to tune in to God through what you hear from others in the meeting. As well as telling the others in the group what happened in your prayer, you might like to share with them some of the times when you were aware of tuning in to God's presence. If there is time and in order to deepen the reflection, you could discuss what sort of liturgical prayer for the parish or group would help you and others to tune in to God.

6
Holiness and Wholeness— Getting beneath the Shell

Our growth in prayer, faith, and holiness will require that we live out of our true selves and break through the shell that we all create to protect ourselves. Part of us has to die if we are to become fully alive. Dismantling our protective shell can be a painful process, but it is worthwhile because it lets us grow and gives others a glimpse of the unique creation that each of us is.

The natural world is full of complex self-defense mechanisms. Some living beings survive by speed of movement, or by donning some form of camouflage or disguise. Others hope they can protect themselves with tough outer coatings, such as the prickles on a hedgehog or the hard shells covering snails, tortoises, and many delicate sea creatures. These self-defense mechanisms have developed over thousands or even millions of years. They exist to protect the life of the creature, to keep predators away, to let the species survive. They tell the whole world, "Here is something very precious, very tasty, very delicate, very beautiful. Here is something that is the core of my life and yet is very vulnerable. So, keep your distance. Don't invade my space. I am going to do my utmost to keep you out!"

I am not an expert in psychology, but I have reflected on my own feelings and I have observed the way other human beings live and survive. From these observations, rather than from any academic standpoint, I offer a few thoughts that may help to throw some light on the way we are. In turn, understanding ourselves can lead us to know God and God's workings better.

My first observation is that, like most living things, we human beings also create protective self-defense mechanisms around ourselves. These are not physical barriers but psychological, intellectual, and spiritual ones. Our instincts tell us that our main adversaries will be people who can hurt us deep down by subtle words and actions. We are less afraid of being hurt physically.

What is it that we are so eager to defend? What are we afraid might happen to us if we don't defend it? Many people will be aware that hidden deep within the heart of each person there is a reality that is very beautiful and totally unique. It is very difficult to describe exactly what this is. Some would say that it is the childlike side of us, others that it is Godlike. While it is hard to put our finger on it, we are aware that it is something very beautiful, very precious, and very vulnerable. It is "the real me," the core of my being, the particular something that makes me a special and unique individual. It is the part of me that is deepest and most hidden, the heart that can love and receive love. It is something so precious that it seems somehow to be for all time and into eternity.

If you watch the way babies grow and develop through infancy and early childhood, you will see how they soon begin to learn that their special individuality needs a certain amount of protection. Particularly at times of interaction with older brothers and sisters and with other children, they spend much of their time trying to build a protective wall or shell around their beautiful inner self.

On reflection, it is easy to see why this is so, although at the time there is no conscious awareness of what is going on. Deep down most of us are afraid that if we allow other people to see our real selves, they will betray and destroy this beauty with ridicule and gossip. We cannot bear to think of anyone treating the deepest and most precious core of our self in that way. Like so many creatures in the natural world, we therefore have to decide how to throw people off the scent and keep them away from finding our hidden beauty.

Our best means of defense is to create and then hide behind an image that we portray to others. This image will often be modeled on the way we see other people act, a type of "role model." Initially, our parents and immediate family provide these role models. Later, especially after we have started school, the effect of the peer group begins to make itself felt. Later still, new ways of acting and of responding to situations are based on other significant people. Some role models may emerge from the situations we see on television or read about in comics, magazines, and newspapers. Soap operas, for example, can lead us to act in the same ways as the characters we see. Modeling ourselves on these "role models" helps us to live in a way that we imagine will be acceptable to others.

All this can be observed by watching the behavior of a young person through childhood and adolescence. What has happened is that each in his or her own way has created a shell to protect the deeper self. We have all done this in our time of growing up. This shell is not our true self, but it is all we allow other people to see.

Throughout adult life, through the circumstances and situations in which we find ourselves, we constantly have to make choices. On the one hand, we can make choices that come out of and reinforce our "shell," created in the image and likeness of acceptability. It may even come to the point that we completely forget that any other deeper "self" exists at all. On the other hand, we can make choices out of our real self, the self created in the image and likeness of God.

These choices will sometimes be associated with the major milestones of life—bereavement, serious illness in ourselves or in a loved one, a broken relationship, a change of job or lifestyle, retirement or redundancy, falling in love, leaving home. At these times, we respond to the situation or crisis either by retreating further into our shell or by letting our true self come more to the fore. When we do the latter, we sometimes describe it as "facing up to ourselves." This is exactly what we have to do when we are confronted by some of these major milestones of life, and it is through these situations that our "shell" is weakened.

The ordinary events of everyday life can also help us to reveal more of our true self. We gently let our real self emerge in an act of kindness or a job well done. Sometimes we notice this at times of beauty: the song of a bird, music, a work of art. Even during an argument or disagreement, or when we are let down or misunderstood, there are opportunities for letting our real self grow.

"Coming out of our shell" to make these choices will often involve a degree of suffering. The right choice may not be the easy option. Choosing to be what God created us to be will lead ultimately to a greater sense of fulfillment and peace. This is not always easy to appreciate as we are faced with the more immediate prospects of pain and hardship. Letting go of our protective shell is a painful process. It means we are vulnerable, open to ridicule, exposed. It involves many dark nights, many false hopes, and great courage. It requires that we put our trust completely in God's love for us, let go of our safety nets, and step out into the dark. These are moments of great grace because they are the times when God is calling us to peel off another layer of our shell. That means becoming more as we were made to be.

The process of breaking through our false outer shell in order to find our real self can come about in different ways, which can be described with the help of some simple images. In the first place, we can talk about dismantling our shell. To dismantle something is a slow, gradual process. It does not have to be violent or painful. It can be quite gentle and unassuming. But progress has to be made, and we need to keep working at it. Going on retreat, reflecting on the Scriptures, praying, being kind and good in small things—these are all ways in which our shell will be gradually dismantled.

Another description is that it is like peeling away the layers of an onion or taking the skin from a banana. This also implies a gradual and gentle process over a considerable time, but it contains the suggestion of something more painful. This may happen, for example, when we cope with what are sometimes described as the crosses of life, or put up with some niggling illness and pain, or accept other people even when they are difficult.

There are, of course, other ways of getting through an outer shell. We can take a hammer to it! We can crush it underfoot. These are violent ways that may end up destroying the beautiful creature inside at the same time. Sometimes it feels like this when something devastating happens to us. A bereavement, a sudden illness, a broken relationship—we feel as though we are being cracked open by nutcrackers. In these situations, "shattered" would be a better word to use than "dismantled."

Dismantling, peeling away the layers, shattering—all these images depict the destruction of our self-created shell. But what images and ideas can be used to portray how our real self is growing at the same time?

Imagine going into a dark room in the early morning and pulling back the curtains to let the daylight in. The dark murky interior is suddenly bathed in color and light. Within the room we see everything clearly, we can move about freely. We can also look out through the window and see the sky and the view. We can notice what sort of day it is. We see that the world extends beyond our little room and that it is a beautiful and amazing world. In the same way, allowing the curtains that cover our real self to be pulled back will reveal the color and texture of what is inside us. It will enable us to see things clearly and to make decisions freely. It will also give us a new and broader perspective with which to look at our world. It will equip us to see things in a new light. In the natural world this may be a move toward a more contemplative view of nature and beauty. In society it will help us to see things in perspective, to make more informed decisions, to discern and recognize the signs of the kingdom of God.

All this is what we call holiness. A good description of holiness is allowing the curtains to be drawn back to reveal our deepest self. It means letting the light of Christ shine into us, in the same way that the light floods into a room when the curtains are drawn back. True holiness will help us to be truer to our real self and will also give us a new and broader outlook on the world.

The dismantling of our false self and the emergence of our deeper self are the two sides of the same coin. They are good for us, and they are also necessary for other people. The real reason for holiness is not simply that we become better for our own sakes, nor is it just to get us to heaven. The real purpose of God's gift is for the continuing creation of a better world. Our self-discovery is a gift to those about us, our family, friends, neighbors, and colleagues. We will be much nicer people to be with if we live out of our true self and not out of the false protective shell.

Living out of our true inner self will reveal God to others because, whereas our shell is created by us, our true self is the unique creation of God. If that unique revelation of God that is me lies dormant and hidden, then the whole world will be impoverished. What a responsibility we have to let others see us as God made us!

For Personal Prayer

As before, refer to the pattern in the introduction. The grace you might like to ask for in this prayer is the gift of having the courage to let God dismantle your "shell" and allow others to see your real inner self. Alternatively, you may find you simply want to ask for the grace of true holiness.

Scripture

In the conversation with Nicodemus in Saint John's Gospel (3:1–21) Jesus describes how someone must be "born again" if they are to enter the kingdom of God. Slowly read these few phrases and be conscious of what God may be asking you.

> There was one of the Pharisees called Nicodemus, a leading Jew, who came to Jesus by night....Jesus answered: "I tell you most solemnly, unless a man is born from above, he cannot see the kingdom of God." Nicodemus said, "How can a grown man be born? Can he go back into his mother's womb and be born again?" Jesus replied: "...unless a man is born through water and the Spirit, he cannot enter the kingdom of God: what is born of the flesh is flesh: what is born of the Spirit is spirit....On these grounds is sentence pronounced: that though the light has come into the world men have shown they prefer darkness to the light because their deeds were evil. And indeed, everybody who does wrong hates the light and avoids it, for fear his actions should be exposed; but the man who lives by the truth comes out into the light, so that it may be plainly seen that what he does is done in God."

To Help Your Reflection

- How did I feel as I read this chapter? Did it "ring bells" with me? When do I put up protective barriers, and when do I find I don't need them?
- Nicodemus came by night—he had something to hide. He is afraid of the ridicule and laughter of his friends and neighbors, his fellow Pharisees, if he admits that he is interested in Jesus. When I work out of my false self, am I also furtive and ashamed? Am I afraid of the ridicule of others if I show my true colors? What am I trying to hide?
- To be his true self, Nicodemus needs to discard the protective shell of respectability he has put around himself and be "born again." He needs to return to the innocence and openness of babyhood. What elements have I built into a protective shell around myself? What do I need to discard if I am to return to a childlike innocence?
- Can I recall any situation in my life that has felt like pulling back the curtains to let the light in? Was I aware of the light of Christ coming into my life?

In a Listening Group

When you are ready to start, recall the pattern on page xxii. You may like to put a few seashells on the table near the candle to help everyone focus on the idea of protective shells. The grace you could ask for is for the courage for each of us to be true to our self.

How much can be shared in this very personal topic will depend on each individual. It is necessary to remember in every meeting that everything we hear as we listen to the others must always remain completely confidential. At the same time, everyone must be free to share as little or as much as he or she wants.

To deepen the reflection, you might like to reflect together on how hard it is to share with others something of ourselves and how much we need to trust others.

7
Prayer—
From the Hidden Depths within Us

In many sermons and books, prayer is described as being like a conversation. This can imply that God is somehow separate and apart. While not denying that this is an important viewpoint, I want to investigate in this chapter what our prayer can be like if we start from the understanding that God is present within us.

Hidden in the hills of north Wales, away from the tourist trails and well off the beaten track, is a reservoir. It is situated at the center of a large natural bowl with gently sloping sides. The immediate surroundings are scrubland, but the bowl, which covers an area of several square miles, is extensive and bare, with a few sheep, rabbits, and small birds the only signs of life. This is not a big, important reservoir serving a city or large conurbation, but a small supply that provides water for a couple of farms. It is about twice the size of a large swimming pool. It is not even important enough to have a name—maps of the area simply mark it "res." Even the few marked footpaths stop short before they reach it.

Although hardly noticeable, even from relatively

nearby, closer inspection reveals that the reservoir has a character of its own. At one end, the dam that has been built is strong and well made, holding back the water with quarried stones covered in low grass and moss. The sloping inside wall is also faced with well-laid stonework. There is abundant evidence that considerable time and effort has gone into constructing this reservoir. It was clearly intended to last.

On the three sides of the reservoir where there is rising ground, several small streams trickle down the hillsides to replenish the supply. These streams gather water from a large area, channeling it to where it can be put to use. On the fourth side of the reservoir is a pipe, presumably taking the water to its destination. And between the inflow and outflow of the water are the dark, silent depths of the reservoir itself. The surface of the water, well sheltered below the level of the surrounding rim, is hardly ruffled by the passing breeze. The sloping sides of the reservoir lead the eye beneath the calm surface, hinting at unimaginable depths beyond.

This description of a small reservoir can be useful as a way of describing what the grace of God and prayer are like. We can compare God's grace with a huge reservoir that never runs dry and liken prayer to the process of tapping into it. In this chapter I want to take a slightly different perspective, starting from the fact that God is present in all things. Rather than thinking of the reservoir as something outside yourself, I invite you to imagine a small reservoir inside your heart. As this idea develops, I want to explore what light it can shed on our understanding of prayer.

Our starting point is the fact that God creates everything and is present at the heart of all. I have mentioned already that God is like a big embrace, enfolding and including everything that is; God is like a circle, enclosing the whole of the universe. Each of us is created out of a different place in this circle. It is as though a small piece of the divinity was chipped off to make each of us, and this is reflected in our individuality. Each of us is a "chip off the old block." In each individual, a different aspect of God finds form; each human being incarnates something unique about God. Imagine the unique reservoir deep within your heart, an individual reflection of divine life that is special to you. Like the reservoir of water, hidden from view except at close quarters, the inmost self of each person is hidden and secret. Like the reservoir, it may be well camouflaged, overgrown with plants and bushes, with no signposts to point the way. Only someone very close to us can discover this part of us and even this discovery barely ruffles the surface, leaving the dark and silent depths to remain a mystery.

We can never understand this mystery, even though it is so much part of us, but accepting that it is true will affect the way we pray and our whole understanding of prayer. Prayer will no longer be like a conversation face-to-face with an unseen deity; it will be much more a matter of delving into and exploring the depths within us. Our prayer will begin with an acknowledgment of what we are inside, rather than where we are in relation to another. Picture the reservoir deep within; our primary task in prayer will be to reach down into the depths to acknowledge our hidden resources.

A second understanding of prayer will be that it is something that feeds and sustains our inner reservoir, like the streams that trickle down the hillside, gathering water from the surrounding area and channeling it into the reservoir. There will be many different aspects to this prayer, all of them important as sources of life and replenishment for our inner self. These different aspects of prayer may include formal prayer, liturgical prayer, charismatic prayer, scriptural prayer, meditation, and so on. All these, and other types of prayer, are sources of sustenance that are vital because, like the reservoir, there is a danger of becoming stagnant if our feeder streams dry up.

These streams flowing into our inner selves are also links with a wider and more complex system. The reservoir is part of a vast cyclical ecosystem. Water evaporates into clouds that drop their moisture as rain. This seeps through the ground, picking up mineral deposits. Some of this water evaporates again to repeat the cycle, other parts of it are used to give nourishment to the vegetation, and so on. There are many different parts of creation that are touched and given life in abundance by this complex system. It is almost as though the reservoir is linked to the whole of creation and seems at one with the entire universe. So it is with prayer, which links us into a network of spirituality, which could be described as goodness, holiness, or oneness with God. When we pray, the sustenance we receive is linked and connected with every other person. For believers there is an additional special link of faith that Christians describe in the Creed as "the communion of saints." It is very consoling and gives great confidence to know that the strength, support, and nourishment we receive when we pray is linked to this vast network of spiritual strength.

Of course, the reservoir not only receives water, it also

has an outlet that channels the water to where it is needed. In fact, the whole purpose of the reservoir is to be a channel to direct the streams to their final destination. This leads us to a third aspect of prayer. The unique reservoir of divine life within us is not principally for our own benefit but is directed outward for the good of others. The outflow of God's life from our hearts may be shown in different ways. Caring for other people and ministering to them are obvious examples. Teaching, bringing up a family, working for justice and peace, creative work in the arts—these are some of the means by which the life of God is channeled from us to others. Remember, all people, not just those with religious faith, have a unique part of God's life in them. That is why goodness and creativeness are not exclusive to religious people and are seen in people of all faiths or none. The special task of those with an active religious faith is to recognize and point out the life of God as it is manifested in themselves and in others. For these people, an important outflow from their reservoir will be this "naming" of the presence of God.

The outflow of God's life from our reservoir is particularly evident and true when we consider prayers of intercession. We sometimes imagine this prayer to be like going into the presence of a mighty king to bow down and plead for mercy or help for someone. We think of ourselves as standing in the presence of the all-powerful God on behalf of someone who is sick or troubled or in need of our intercession for some reason. But this prayer of intercession can also be thought of as holding the other person within our inner self, being in solidarity with them. When we pray for another person, we reach down into the depths within us, depths that are linked to the whole communion of saints, and on their behalf we draw out the strength contained there.

Because the reservoir in each of us is an individual creation, the prayer of each of us will also be unique. It is quite remarkable to realize that everyone's prayer comes from a different corner of the Divine, out of a unique part of the universal embrace of God. Inasmuch as each of us is faithful to God's life in us and applies that life to others, so will the world be more as God created it to be. If any one of us fails to recognize, respond to, and nurture the life of God in us, the whole world will be poorer. Then the opportunity for each person's particular and unique revelation of God to come to fruition will be lost for eternity, and there will never again be another chance. To use another example, the presence of God in our world is rather like a jigsaw puzzle in which each of us is a single unique piece. The more pieces that fit into place, the more the whole picture takes shape. Pieces that fail to find their rightful place leave a gap that no other piece can fill.

I have mentioned three aspects of prayer in this chapter. First, prayer is the process of becoming more conscious of the singular creation that I am, and becoming more aware of the presence of God in my heart. Second, prayer is the receiving of sustenance and strength from the myriad experiences of my daily life. Finally, prayer is the outflow of new life from my reservoir to the world. In this dynamic of prayer, the inflow and the outflow have to be balanced. Too much inflow with nothing allowed out, and the water will flow uselessly out of the overflow; too much outflow with insufficient new input, and the reservoir eventually runs dry. If there is neither inflow or outflow, the water will become stagnant and lifeless.

What I have described in this chapter may be a new idea to many people. My purpose has been to show that our relationship with God, and particularly our prayer, is much larger than the narrow confines into which we sometimes put it. How we pray will depend largely on where we think God is. It may well be that you are happy with your prayer and the way you pray, in which case I would urge you to continue. Pray as you can, not as you can't. But it may be that you find prayer difficult, dry, and somewhat frustrating. If so, the time may be right to try something new. My hope is that the ideas in this chapter will help to provide a new direction and open up new possibilities as we each continue our journey into the mystery of God.

For Personal Prayer

You might like to think back to the points in this chapter and ask God for a particular grace for your prayer. It may be that you would want to ask for the grace to be able to go deeper in your prayer.

Scripture

The prayer of Christ at the Last Supper, often known as the priestly prayer of Christ, includes many phrases that tell us of the involvement of the life of the Trinity within us. While the prayer "That they all may be one" is often used to refer to the desire for unity between the churches, a much deeper application implies a prayer that we will be one with God. Read the following phrases in the light of the reservoir of divine life in your heart. Read the phrases slowly several times so that their meaning sinks in. They are all from the seventeenth chapter of Saint John's Gospel.

"...And eternal life is this:
to know you,
the only true God,
and Jesus Christ whom you have sent.
...Holy Father,
keep those you have given me true to your name,
so that they may be one like us.
...They do not belong to the world
any more than I belong to the world,
consecrate them in the truth;
your word is truth.
...I pray not only for these,
but for those also
who through their words will believe in me.
May they all be one.
Father, may they be one in us,
as you are in me and I am in you,
so that the world may believe it was you
who sent me.
...With me in them and you in me,
may they be so completely one
that the world will realize it was you who sent me
and that I have loved them as much as you
loved me.
...I have made your name known to them

and will continue to make it known,
so that the love with which you loved me
may be in them,
and so that I may be in them."

To Help Your Reflection

- I imagine the reservoir, hidden and secretive, with water trickling in from the surrounding hillsides, and an outlet pipe. I then imagine God's life in me, unique, special, and individual. What experiences are like the streams flowing into my life, bringing sustenance and growth?
- Jesus' prayer is that all his followers will be one with him and the Father. I imagine God including me and everything in the universe in an enormous embrace. How do I feel to be held in such an embrace?
- I then imagine God to be like a huge jigsaw puzzle. I am one unique piece of this puzzle. How do I feel at being so unique and special?
- Jesus prays for us and for everyone. His prayer is one of solidarity, praying that we may be one. Who do I pray for? What are my most urgent prayers for other people? Can I imagine my prayer as holding the person or people I am praying for in my heart? What does the communion of saints mean to me?

In a Listening Group

Remind yourself of the grace you asked for in your personal prayer and share this with the group. You may want to put a bowl of water near the candle in the center of the group to help people recall the idea of a reservoir. To deepen the reflection, you could talk about how you understand prayer for others, prayer of intercession. And you might like to discuss what it feels like to consider your parish/group as a "communion of saints."

8
The Scriptures—
Where We Make Our Home

Home is the place where we can most truly be ourself. As we have seen, faith is a journey with constant movement, but human nature also needs stability and a place of safety and rest. In this chapter I look at how and where we can find this stability in the midst of our changing and sometimes uncertain journey through life.

What is it that enables us to go into certain situations and immediately feel at home? Is it the friendliness of the welcome, the sight of familiar faces, the feeling of being loved and valued?

It is all these things and more. Home means comfy slippers, our favorite armchair to sink into, a cozy fireside during winter storms. Home implies laughter and happiness, friendship and love, the murmurings of grandparents and the shrill cry of children. In reality, we may live in a small flat, a terraced house, a large semi- or detached house; our dwelling may be shared, rented, or owned. But wherever we live and whatever our circumstances, if it is home, then it is our palace.

Feeling at home is quite different from the feeling we

have when we go into other situations and immediately know we are "not at home." We are uneasy as we walk through the door of a strange pub or restaurant and imagine that the level of conversation suddenly drops and that we are the object of myriad staring eyes. We feel self-conscious and awkward when we go to a meeting or party and don't know anyone, and we shuffle around hoping that someone, anyone, will talk to us. We are apprehensive when we arrive in an unfamiliar town on holiday with nowhere to stay and not knowing our way around. We feel uncomfortable, unsure, and ill at ease in strange surroundings until we become familiar with them.

Jesus has some very powerful words about what and where our home can be. "If you make my word your home," he says in Saint John's Gospel (8:31–32), "you will indeed be my disciples, you will learn the truth and the truth will make you free."

Making the word of God our home will be a new idea to many people. What could Jesus possibly have meant? We are used to the idea of taking the word of God *into* our home. Many people do that through reading the Scriptures and through prayer. But actually making the word of God our home—that is something quite markedly different.

How are we to go about making the word of God our home and becoming ever more familiar with it? It is important to stress in the first place that knowing and loving the Bible does not imply that we need to be very clever. Deep insights into the Scriptures can come from people who have little or no formal education in Bible studies. Nor does it imply that we need to take up a serious course of Bible study, although, as we grow in love of God's word, we may well find that we want to know more of the background. The intellectual study of the Scriptures certainly has its uses, and it can help a great deal toward making the Scriptures our home, but it is not the be-all and end-all. In fact, it is even possible to study the Scriptures in great depth and never end up becoming closer to God.

So, what is the most important element in our approach to the Scriptures in order to make them our home? The most fundamental consideration is learning to use the Scriptures for prayer and personal reflection. My introduction at the beginning of this book explains how this can be done, and the section for personal prayer at the end of each chapter gives an opportunity to put this into practice. Becoming familiar with the Scriptures means that we use them daily for our prayer and inspiration, that we ponder God's word in our hearts, that we believe it is God's word for us.

How many of us can honestly say that we have made the word of God our home? And if we are in any doubt about it, a crucial test is to ask ourselves how we feel about the word of God, the Scriptures, the Bible. When we hear readings from the Bible, do they make us feel comfortable and relaxed, like being at home, or do they make us feel somewhat uneasy, as though we had walked into strange surroundings? When we pick up the Bible, does it feel like walking into our living room or is it, rather, like arriving in an unfamiliar place surrounded by strangers? Most Christians would have to admit to having a long way to go in order truly to make the word of God feel like home.

As we become more familiar with the way God speaks

to us in the Scriptures, we should be aware of certain blind alleys that can divert us from the right path. For example, it is not helpful to take everything in the Bible literally as though it were all historically accurate. There are many contradictions in the Bible, and if a particular verse strikes us, we should not immediately think it is literally true. Later, we may find another verse that contradicts it, and that will lead to confusion. Understanding the various types of "truth" in the Bible is crucial. Prayer, careful discernment, and great humility are needed if we are to be truly guided by the Scriptures. Nor can we expect to pick up the Bible and instantly find answers to our problems. One of the reasons why some people find the Scriptures difficult is that they expect them to contain magical formulas that can be prescribed for all our spiritual ills, rather like the prescription the doctor gives us to make us physically better. There are no instant solutions, marvelous one-line cures, or shortcuts to salvation in the Bible. Hoping for these things will only lead to frustration.

Making the Scriptures our home is quite different from these instant solutions or flashes of inspirational lightning. It is like finding the presence of God in a constant gentle breeze rather than in the heart of a sudden storm. It is over time that we grow in our love of the Scriptures, in the same way that it takes time for a house or neighborhood really to feel like home. Familiarity with the word of God is built up over a long period, and in this way it gradually becomes our home. Why does it take this length of time? Because really to feel at home, a new place has to be tried and tested, so that all the uncertainties are ironed out and it feels safe and secure. Gradually, without our noticing it, the Scriptures become like an old and much loved pair of bedroom slippers—comfortable, relaxing, well used, and the place to which we long to return.

"Home," as the saying goes, "is where the heart is." It is our base camp from where we go out to our daily encounters with the world and where we return when we want rest and refreshment. Home is where we recharge our batteries, reenergize ourselves—where we receive strength and sustenance.

Home is also a place of safety, where we can let the barriers down and still feel unthreatened. It is our castle, where we are monarchs and rulers of all we survey, where nobody can intrude upon us, and where we can control who comes and goes and how long they stay. It is a place where we can be ourselves, let our hair down, make fools of ourselves—and still know that people will value, love, and respect us.

When the word of God starts to become our home, it will be the source of all these things for us too. It will be our base camp, which gives us strength and energy to face up to our daily tasks, whatever they might be. And after we have been busy with all sorts of concerns and tasks, it will be in the Scriptures that we will find rest and recuperation. In the Scriptures we will find that we are completely safe and that at the times when we are being our most ridiculous selves, we will know for certain that we are valued, loved, and cherished by God.

"If you make my word your home," says Jesus, "you will indeed be my disciples; you will learn the truth and the truth will make you free" (John 8:31–32).

Saint John's Gospel has a further surprise in store. Not only are we to make our home in God's word, but God will also make his home in us: "If anyone loves me he will keep my word, and my Father will love him, and we shall come to him and make our home in him" (John 14:23).

Think again about all the things that "home" brings to mind, then realize that all these things are what God hopes to find in each of us. A place of familiarity. Certainly we would expect God to be familiar with us. But what of comfort? Does God really feel relaxed and comfortable within us? And safety? For God to feel safe and secure within us is extraordinary. In these words, Jesus is actually inviting us to think of ourselves as God's favorite, comfy bedroom slippers! Wow!

The Father, Son, and Spirit live in us, not just in a superficial way, but really and truly they make their home in us. God makes a home in us not just for our own well-being and satisfaction. God's purpose is to bring to fulfillment the salvation and redemption of the world. In other words, this home that is ourselves is God's base camp from where the world will be transformed.

There is one further phrase in St. John's Gospel that brings both these ideas together: "Make your home in me, as I make mine in you" (15:4). This homemaking is mutual. God makes a home in us, lives in us, is comfortable and safe in us, and we are the base camp for God's action in the world. We, in our turn, make our home in God, in God's word, in the Scriptures. As our familiarity with God's word grows, so does it become our home, our castle, the place where our heart is.

Notice, it is God who makes a home in us first. The result and consequence of this action of God is that we make our home in God's word. The temptation is to think that if we are good and work hard and pray well and learn to make the Scriptures our home, then God will come to live in us—almost as though this was the reward for all our efforts. But actually it is the other way around. God is the one who does all the hard work in us first. As a result of God's presence, we are inspired and encouraged to make our home in God's word. And so the cycle is continually repeated—when God is home in us, our free response is to become more familiar with the word of God, as it penetrates more deeply into our lives, and in turn God becomes more intensely present in us. It is thus that we are drawn in a spiral ever more profoundly into the mystery of God. That is the heart of our adventure.

For Personal Prayer

The grace you might like to ask for is to be able to understand and love the Scriptures better or to have God show you how to be at home with God's word.

Scripture

There have been several references to Scripture passages in this chapter, and a quiet reflection on these phrases would be beneficial. Alternatively, a passage of Scripture that incorporates many of these ideas in a slightly different context is the parable of the vine and the branches (John 15:1–17). Read these verses, or the whole of this section, in your Bible, slowly and prayerfully. Read it two or three times, and notice any words or phrases that stand out for you.

"I am the true vine,
and my Father is the vinedresser.
Every branch in me that bears no fruit
he cuts away,
and every branch that does bear fruit he prunes
to make it bear even more.
You are pruned already,
by means of the word that I have spoken to you.
Make your home in me, as I make mine in you.
As a branch cannot bear fruit all by itself,
but must remain part of the vine,
neither can you unless you remain in me.
I am the vine,
you are the branches.
…If you remain in me
and my words remain in you,
you may ask what you will
and you shall get it.
…I call you friends,
because I have made known to you
everything I have learnt from my Father."

To Help Your Reflection

- How do I feel about the ideas I've read in this chapter? Where or when do I feel "at home" with God?
- How do I feel about the idea of being one of the branches on God's vine? Does my prayer reflect the fact that I am part of the vine? Have there been any occasions when I have felt cut off from the vine? What do I do to make sure that my links with the vine are firm and certain?

- What is the place of Scripture in my life? Do I feel at home with the Bible?
- How does it feel to know that God wants to be home in me? Am I going to invite God in? Is there any way I can make my life more "homely" for God?

In a Listening Group

As well as telling the group what happened in your prayer time, you might like to relate some occasion when the word of God in the Scriptures has struck you and made a difference to you. To help with this, place an open Bible near the candle during your time of prayer together. Remember to give everyone the time and space to tell their experiences.

If there is time, you may want to discuss the following questions. But remember what you have learned about listening. Don't interrupt one another, and make sure that everyone has a chance to speak. If your point of view is different from someone else's, remember that it doesn't necessarily mean that they (or you) are wrong, simply that you differ. It's good to hear different opinions, and the group does not need to come to a common conclusion about everything, so allow a lot of freedom in the sharing.

- What are the differences between Bible "study" and "praying" the Bible? Has anyone tried to do either? If not, do you want to start? What steps might that involve? If anyone has studied and prayed the Bible, how can you develop this further?
- How does God use each of us as a base camp for the evangelization of the people around us?

9
Life, Death, and Regeneration

The natural rhythm of the seasons provides a parallel with the rhythm of our spiritual life. Death—regeneration—new life. All living things grow old and finally come to an end. But even in death itself, there are the seeds of new life in abundance for the future. In this chapter I look at how this pattern applies to our relationship with God as expressed in our faith and our prayer, and to our relationship with others in our church communities.

Most of us take the seasons of the year very much for granted. The rhythms of nature are familiar to us. We know that spring follows hard on the heels of winter; the abundance of summer leads to the subtle tints and mellowness of autumn. We have ceased to be amazed by the certainty and wonder of the seasons.

An alien who dropped in from another planet and who knew nothing of seasons would have a quite different view. Imagine what it would be like arriving on our planet at the end of November or in the dark, dank days of December. Alien eyes would no doubt boggle at the sight of Christmas festivities. But apart from that, the scene of apparently lifeless vegetation would imply that here is a world that is in the final throes of death. Late autumn and winter is a time of endings. Leaves have fallen off the trees, the ground is lifeless and sodden, birds have ceased their song. Even the hours of daylight become shorter and shorter. Everywhere there are signs of death and decay. It is easy to imagine that the end is not far away.

Of course, we know better than the alien who has just dropped in. We are not worried about the lifelessness that surrounds us because we know for sure that spring is just around the corner. We have seen it all before. We know it will happen again. Come April and May there will be a new abundance of color and growth and life. We know from experience it has always been so. There is not the slightest doubt that it will happen again. We also know, because science tells us, that throughout the winter months, nature is regenerating itself. Hidden far below the surface, new life is forming. As yet, we cannot see any signs of it, but we know that it is there all the same. Winter is the time when nature is taking a breather and getting ready for the next big effort in the spring. Vegetation is having a rest before its glory days of blossom and flower and abundance in the spring. Animal life, too, is resting, ready for its time of reproduction, nest building, raising young families. Just as we all need the hours of rest and sleep each day to renew us and give us fresh energy, so does the whole natural world need its annual time of rest and regeneration.

Death and decay lead into rest and regeneration, which in turn give birth to renewed and vigorous activity. This physical rhythm of the seasons, and of our daily time scale, is repeated in the spiritual reality of our lives. In fact, understanding this rhythm can shed light on some of the most important realities of our lives—prayer and faith, the Church, death and bereavement.

Let us begin by reflecting on our relationship with God in prayer and in what we describe as our faith. Most people, as they progress in spiritual matters, experience times in prayer that could be described as akin to autumn and winter. "My prayer isn't what it used to be" is a familiar cry. Prayer becomes hard work; we grow lethargic and uninterested; we feel as though we are getting nowhere and there is no point in it any more. Every attempt to pray seems doomed to failure; there is no light at the end of the tunnel; the "autumnal" feeling of death and decay pervades the whole of our prayer and belief. God seems a long way away. And the worst of it is, the more we struggle and try to conjure up the old feelings, the harder it gets. We wonder if there is any point in it after all. We feel like giving up altogether.

Saint John of the Cross described this reality in very vivid terms and called it the "dark night of the soul." His description often puts ordinary Christians off. It sounds as though it is only for very holy people. I believe that this "dark night of the soul" is the experience of most people as they make progress in prayer and in their journey to God. If our faith and our prayer are to be living and growing, some sort of "dark night" will be a necessary part of our development. It is not extraordinary. It is the lot of most good and sincere Christians.

Why should this be a necessary part of our growth? One explanation is that if we keep to our faith and our prayer simply because it makes us feel good, then there is at least some element of selfishness in our motives. Having to go through a difficult time means we focus more on

God and pray for God's sake, not for the nice feelings we can get out of it. Another explanation, in keeping with our autumnal theme, is that there has to be an autumn and a winter in our prayer before there can be spring. In other words, during the darkest part of the night, new life, unseen and unheralded, is beginning to form. We can expect that after the darkness, the new life will be more abundant and wonderful than we could ever have imagined.

Many people will be able to recognize elements of the "dark night" in their experience of prayer and faith. Some may say that their prayer seems like a dark night all of the time! In practice, this "dark night" will be experienced in different ways. Some will feel they are suddenly plunged into a darkness where all attempts to pray and to have any sense of faith disappear. For others, it will be more like clouds passing across the sky, in which periods of darkness are interspersed with times of light.

It is little consolation to say that these experiences of darkness in faith and prayer can last for many years—even, sometimes, for a lifetime. It may be more consoling to compare these times with the seasonal autumn and winter, when regeneration finds its roots and when the new shoots of spring begin to be formed. Before there can be the new growth of spring, there has to be the winter time of rest and recuperation, when it seems as if nothing is happening.

Almost every aspect of our lives has echoes of this seasonal rhythm. As well as helping us to understand the rhythms of our prayer, it may also have something to say to our communities—churches as a whole and local parish communities.

An alien who dropped in on the Church in the Western

world today might be forgiven for concluding that winter has set in. The alien would see parishes dozing, falling numbers of clergy, young people leaving in droves, and a general sense of "the end of an era." A cursory glance over the ecclesiastical scene, concentrating solely on numbers, would indicate that the mainstream churches are on a downward slope. But just as our experience of the seasons tells us that there is new life after the winter, so with the Church our knowledge of the past together with the promises of Christ are solid reasons for hope in the future.

Just as in nature you have to look very closely to see the signs of new growth, so in the Church close inspection will reveal the hidden signs of new life and growth that are the seeds of a new spring. What are these signs? One of the main ones is a deeper sense of personal spirituality rooted in a greater understanding of the Scriptures that so many people have. There is also the increase of faith-sharing groups, prayer groups, and small base communities. There is the growing commitment to follow the call of baptism and an awareness that one of the implications of this is to be increasingly involved in lay and collaborative ministry. The list could go on. Certainly, the signs of a new and exciting life are there if our friendly alien were to scratch below the visible surface.

These signs are present in all the main Christian churches. To a greater or lesser degree they are also present in many local parishes. Here are found the seeds of future growth—deeper prayer, renewed commitment to faith, and a growing awareness of the essential link between faith and everyday life. In God's good time, a new spring will come with a great blossoming of spiritual vitality. The deepening spirituality in so many individuals and communities is the seedbed from which this new growth will develop.

Nature's seasonal rhythms of death, regeneration, and new life can help us understand many of the deep realities of our lives. They give insights into the patterns in our prayer and into our community life. These rhythms of nature also help to explain the Christian attitude to the great mystery that affects us all—the question of death and what happens after death.

It is a strange paradox that new life and regeneration can come about only if it is preceded by death. Around a fallen and rotting tree, new forms of life grow up; the dead carcasses of animals become food for others; dead leaves and other vegetation provide the nutrients for a new generation of life. And, most obvious of all, the seed has to die if it is to give birth to a new plant or tree. This is the example used in the gospels by Jesus himself. "Unless a seed falls to the ground and dies, it remains a single grain. But if it dies it yields a rich harvest." It is almost as though he is saying, "The greatest moment of glory for the seed, the moment for which it was created, is when it stops being itself and becomes something else."

Implicit in the words of Jesus was his own death and resurrection. He frequently warned his followers that he would have to suffer and die. He pointed out how the prophets had foreseen that the Christ should die. If he was to overcome death, he first had to die. Only then would new life be possible. There are several occasions in the gospels when Jesus seems frustrated because his disciples are so slow to understand the inevitability of his impending death.

Death is the one certainty of life. Bereavement, the loss

of a close loved one, is something that everyone has to go through. The death of a parent, a partner, one's own child, or a very close friend is a traumatic experience. It is no exaggeration to say that a part of us dies with the death of someone close. But every death contains within it the possibilities of new life.

The words of the Roman Catholic funeral service sum it up: "Lord, for your faithful people, life is changed, not ended." The seed dying to give new life; a person's death leading to a new eternity. It is no coincidence that the churches remember the dead during the month of November. The end of life in nature, the decay seen in falling leaves, the shortening days of autumn all mirror our remembrance of the death that awaits us. In this way, nature constantly reminds us of our mortality. At the same time, the hope of new life beginning to form deep in the earth reminds us of the promise of new life after death, the pledge of spring as yet unseen, the guarantee of a future that is totally secure.

For Personal Prayer

The grace you could ask for in this prayer may be to understand and accept the rhythms of life, death, and regeneration in your own faith story.

Scripture

The story of the raising of Lazarus in John 11:1–44 is a good example of the rhythm or pattern described above. The full story is longer than the extract given here, and ideally the whole story should be read from the Bible.

Either with the whole story, or with this extract, read the passage slowly and be aware of the thoughts and ideas that strike you.

On arriving, Jesus found that Lazarus had been in the tomb for four days already....Martha said to Jesus, "If you had been here, my brother would not have died, but I know that, even now, whatever you ask of God, he will grant you." "Your brother" said Jesus to her "will rise again." Martha said, "I know he will rise again at the resurrection on the last day." Jesus said, "I am the resurrection. If anyone believes in me, even though he dies he will live, and whoever lives and believes in me will never die."...At the sight of Mary's tears, and those of the Jews who followed her, Jesus said in great distress, with a sigh that came straight from the heart, "Where have you put him?" They said, "Lord, come and see." Jesus wept; and the Jews said, "See how much he loved him!"...Jesus reached the tomb: it was a cave with a stone to close the opening. Jesus said, "Take the stone away."...Jesus cried in a loud voice, "Lazarus, here! Come out!" The dead man came out, his feet and hands bound with bands of stuff and a cloth round his face. Jesus said to them, "Unbind him, let him go free."

To Help Your Reflection

- I imagine myself in the room with Lazarus, Jesus, Martha, and Mary. I notice that they are very open about expressing their feelings. How do I feel as part of this scene?

- What experience have I of bereavement? How easy do I find it to express my feelings when someone close to me has died? In reflecting on my experience, can I identify parallels with the seasons? Can I recognize signs of new life that I found after a bereavement?
- What aspects of my prayer, my faith, my relationships show signs of death and decay? Where are the signs of new growth?
- What attitudes and prejudices need to die in me before new growth can come? What are the things that bind me and hold me down as Lazarus was bound?

In a Listening Group

It is particularly important this time to use a candle. The candle itself may act as a reminder of this theme as the wax has to be burnt up in order to give the flame. In silence recall your time of prayer. When the time for sharing comes, recall the grace you asked for in prayer, and listen to one another without commenting. In particular, and if people think it appropriate, allow time to share some of the painful things about death and bereavement. Great sensitivity will be needed, and remember, it is not a counseling session and not a discussion group. Being with others in prayerful silence and solidarity can be more powerful than words.

If you want to deepen the prayer and have a short discussion, you might talk about the provision that is made in your area for counseling people who are bereaved. But don't let this distract you from tackling the more difficult reflection and sharing.

10
The Frontiers of Faith—
The Mystery of the Sea

Our reflections about God and the mystery of life, death, and eternity may lead us into feelings that can never be adequately described in words. In this chapter I use some of the imagery associated with the sea and show how it can express our deepest feelings.

The Music Hall song "I do like to be beside the seaside" expresses the wish of many people. On holiday weekends we brave hours of crawling traffic to get within sight and sound of the sea, or perhaps we spend fraught hours at airports, waiting to catch often-delayed flights at unsocial hours to reach our holiday home in the sun—invariably by or near the sea.

The sea is like a magnet for people. And because so many people enjoy being by the seaside, it becomes a social, family place. Toddlers roll about in the edge of the water while children chase and splash each other with screams of glee. Grandparents paddle in the shallows, trousers and skirts rolled up to reveal knees white as marble. Teenagers gather in groups around ghetto blasters, flexing their newfound independence like the young

gulls circling far overhead. On bright summer days when
the air is pleasant and the waters comparatively warm,
people come to the beach with chairs, picnic baskets,
windbreaks, towels, beachballs, buckets, and shovels.

But the appeal of the sea is more than simply an ex-
cuse for a day trip or a backdrop to our annual vacation.
There is a sense of mystery and awesomeness that hints
at greater depths and invites us into the contemplation of
things beyond our limited horizons. This has been expressed by countless generations of artists and poets who
have been inspired by the sea. One verse that comes to
mind is that of John Masefield:

> I must go down to the seas again,
> to the lonely sea and the sky.

And there are many other examples from poetry, music,
and the visual arts. What is it about the sea that has inspired so much genius? And why do so many people return to its shores again and again to seek inspiration,
comfort, and solace?

It seems to me that part of the reason is that the sea brings
to mind some of the emotional aspects of life. Unlike
thoughts and ideas, our emotions and feelings are often
difficult to express in words. We know we have them, but
often they are hard to describe because we find that we
are not able to put them into words. But one way in which we
can express our emotions is by using comparisons and parallels. The sea, and everything connected with it, is a powerful source of images to express our every mood. The images
we find there can provide us with the means to express
our feelings and can help us to become more aware of them.

Those who live near the sea and are able to watch it through different seasons will know that it is almost as if the sea has "moods." For example, there are times when the sea is cold and brooding, when white horses play far out in the bay and the gulls are glad to be left in peace. At other times it is stormy and threatening, when people huddle in the promenade cafés and dry sand blown into a frenzy stings bare flesh. Then there are the happy times, sought after and dreamed of by vacationers, when wave after wave chuckles over the sand and bright sunlight is reflected in smiling faces. Balancing all this there are calm, windless days when the sea seems monotonous—placid and unchanging, innocuous and harmless.

Do we recognize some of our own feelings and emotions reflected and mirrored in these different moods of the sea? Fear, anger, joy, peace—these are just a few of our emotions that can be difficult to explain in words yet that can be expressed by comparison with the sea. It is hard to explain in the abstract what our feelings have been; much easier to say, "It felt just like when those great waves come crashing onto the shore..." or "...like those little waves bubbling in at the edge of the sea...."

When we walk or sit by the sea, watching it and reflecting on it, sometimes it can perfectly reflect our mood—stormy and dark in desolation, playful and bright when things are going well. At other times, it is as though the sea is a counterbalance—giving a hint of brightness during dark times or reminding us, when we are feeling on top of the world, that storms may be around the corner. The differing moods of the sea echo much of human life and accurately reflect our feelings and emotions. Small wonder, then, that it has provided inspiration for so many artists and writers and still attracts so many people to-day.

But that still does not fully explain the sense of awe that we feel when we are confronted by the might and majesty of the sea. The sea does not just echo human feelings and emotions, it also hints at greater secrets hidden in its depths. There are glimpses of the mystery of life, and of death. There are even suggestions of new insights into the mystery of God.

To stand on the shore at the edge of the sea is to be on a frontier. Before us, as we look out toward the distant horizon, there is the vast expanse of sea. Where it ends we can hardly imagine. Timeless eternity seems almost tangible as we take in the broad vista. Behind us, there is our own limited world, which may seem very small and insignificant in comparison. As we stand at this frontier, the waters close to us can appear to be like the womb—safe, all-embracing, and comfortable. As our gaze ranges farther toward the horizon, we glimpse the dark depths that may carry hints of the tomb—somber, cold, hidden, and mysterious. In the face of such riddles, life at our frontier, the space between womb and tomb, seems short and fragile.

This mention of frontiers also brings to mind something many children do when they are at the seaside, namely, building a sandcastle. They create a wall of sand around themselves and sit inside it, waiting for the tide to come in. As the water gently laps around, the walls start to crumble. Furious digging ensues. More and more sand is piled on to stop the approaching waters. But in spite of all the industry, the result is inevitable. The fortress they have built is gradually surrounded by the water, and slowly but surely the walls dissolve. No matter how strong the fortress has been, the sea will have its way, and gradually the walls of sand melt back so that only the pristine beach remains.

A falling sandcastle brings to mind the compelling power of the sea, a power also apparent when we listen to the constant deafening roar of the waves and breakers, see mighty waves crashing onto pebbles, or look at cliff faces that have been eaten away by the tide over the years. We know how underlying currents can sweep away even the strongest swimmers. We have heard tales of shipwreck and tidal waves, hurricanes and tornadoes. Even though we are overawed by the power and majesty of the sea, at the same time we are aware that there is gentleness, too, in the ways of the sea. The water lapping around the sandcastle seems to have a soft touch. We know that the tiniest and most delicate creatures make the sea their home. There is an abundance of sustenance for all creatures, from the greatest to the smallest and simplest.

Just as it is no contradiction to say that the sea is powerful and gentle at the same time, so it is with God. The ways of God are like the incoming tide, powerful in its insistence and inevitability, yet gentle and unassuming. This gentle power of God is evident in our lives when we build barriers around ourselves. Like the sandcastle, these barriers are erected to protect ourselves. Because of fear or uncertainty we sometimes don't want God to control our lives, so we build walls of self-sufficiency to hide behind. We busy ourselves with all sorts of "important" things, and we become so preoccupied with the business of living that every hour of every day is fully taken up. Even if we are doing God's work, there may be little time left for him. Our busyness becomes our castle, our safety, our stronghold.

God doesn't attack this fortress with a sledgehammer. God's incursion into our lives is gentle but sure, like the waves lapping around a sandcastle. We hardly notice the little ways in which God is present in our circumstances, our relationships, and our daily lives. This presence is gentle, yet at the same time it is insistent, certain, and inevitable. Sooner or later our walls will crumble. Only when that begins to happen will we be able to be our true selves, the people God created us to be.

The sea has one more truth for us in our journey into the mystery of God. It is the fact that this powerful but gentle God is also totally trustworthy and sure. I was brought up near the seaside town of Morecambe in the northwest of England. At low tide Morecambe Bay becomes a vast expanse of flat sand stretching as far as the eye can see. Part of it can be crossed on foot from Hest Bank to Grange-over-Sands, a distance of six or seven miles. During the summer there are guided walks, but without a guide the crossing is treacherous because of quicksand. Indeed, the story goes that once an entire coach and horses was swallowed up by the quicksand. Nothing was seen of coach, horses, driver, or passengers ever again!

Everyone has to find a true and sure path through life. The way ahead may appear flat and smooth, but below the surface there are hidden dangers. For Christians, the solid ground is found in Christ, the Way, the Truth, and the Life. Guidance toward this solid ground is found in the experience of others who have passed that way before. This may be in the form of the tradition and teaching of the Church, which is the collective experience of those who have followed this way over the centuries. More immediate guidance may come from parents, teachers, religious leaders, and catechists—those who have the wisdom and knowledge to point the way to the firm and solid ground that is Christ.

There are many quicksands to beware of in our modern world. Examples of these are the empty promises of materialism, self-seeking in a consumer society, the lure of drugs, and shallow relationships in which people become disposable when they have served their purpose. The list could go on. Ask any parent, teacher, or religious leader what are the dangers that face young people today and there will be a catalog of the quicksands of our society.

In our rapidly changing world, people need and look for solid and unchanging foundations. The old certainties seem to have gone, and the promises that the new material realities will replace them have not proved to be true. The quicksands of materialism and of the consumer society may appear attractive and safe, but all too often they let people down because there is no true foundation there. The solid foundation must be in God and in God alone. The certainty of the cycles of the sea and of the tidal rhythms reminds us of the sureness of God's love. Nothing is more certain than the constancy of God. If only we could believe that God's love is even more certain than the rhythms of the sea!

For Personal Prayer

The grace you could ask for in this prayer time is to be able to enter more deeply into the mystery of God and eternity.

Scripture

Water is mentioned quite often in Saint John's Gospel. It is symbolic of the new life that Jesus brings. One of the stories that features water is that of Jesus' washing the feet of the disciples (13:1–15). I have chosen this here not because there is any connection with the thoughts about the sea, but because it is in a very true sense an incident that leads us deep into the nature of God. Throughout John's Gospel we have been told, "His hour had not come yet" and "My hour has not yet come." This story begins by saying, "Jesus knew that the hour had come." His "hour" was the moment of the fullest revelation about God, the deepest mystery. This story, therefore, perhaps more than any other, gives us an insight into eternity.

> [Jesus] had always loved those who were his in the world, but now he showed how perfect his love was.... He got up from table, removed his outer garment and, taking a towel, wrapped it round his waist; he then poured water into a basin and began to wash the disciples' feet and to wipe them with the towel he was wearing.

Peter objects to this. He is not going to have Jesus washing his feet. But Jesus tells Peter that, although he may not fully understand, it has to happen, otherwise he can have no part with him.

> When he had washed their feet and put on his clothes again he went back to the table. "Do you understand" he said "what I have done to you? You call

me Master and Lord, and rightly; so I am. If I, then, the Lord and Master, have washed your feet you should wash each other's feet."

To Help Your Reflection

- The sea can provide images that help us to express our feelings. What aspects of the sea best reflect and describe my feelings at present?
- Do I think of God as powerful or as gentle? Do I feel that Jesus' washing of feet expresses both power and vulnerability?
- I imagine myself in the room at the Last Supper with Jesus and the disciples. What does it feel like when Jesus starts to wash our feet? How do I feel as Jesus comes to wash my feet?
- Peter was indignant and tried to stop Jesus from washing his feet. In what areas of my life have I put up barriers to prevent God from ministering to me?

In a Listening Group

Once again, begin by asking for the grace to listen well and recall what happened in your own prayer time. Remember to listen as each person shares what has happened in his or her prayer. You might find it helpful to have a few sea shells or pictures of the sea to remind you of this chapter. To deepen your prayer, you might discuss the different ways in which people you know serve others in the parish or the locality. As this is the last meeting, it would be appropriate to end with some sort of party or celebration. Perhaps other close family members could join for this. Or you might want to hold such a party at a future date when you could review the whole of your time together. However you decide to manage it, the important thing is to end well with a celebration.

Epilogue—
Toward the True Heart
of Evangelization

When I started to prepare and think about this book, I intended it to be a book about evangelization. Those who have read it will probably consider that I have missed the mark by a considerable margin. The word *evangelization* has hardly been mentioned, and only one or two chapters appear to have referred to the subject. However, although the book has been mainly about prayer, faith, and our personal journey, I believe there has been more about evangelization in these chapters than at first meets the eye. I would like to end with a few direct thoughts about what I consider to be the heart of evangelization.

Evangelization is a complex matter. It is not the imposing of the gospel or of a particular religion on other people. It is not some sort of colonization that seeks to take over a person or a group of people. It is not indoctrination, nor is it proselytism. It is not awakening people's spiritual sense in order to control it. It is not even bringing Christ to those who do not know him.

The very word *evangelization* means "good news." The

best news that can be offered to anyone is the realization that every individual is a unique creation, a product of God's imagination. It is the fact, as I have tried to show in this book, that each person makes real, brings to life, or incarnates a different dimension of God, a different corner of the eternal. It is the awareness that each of us is a unique part of the vast embrace of God.

Evangelization, therefore, is not solely about bringing Christ/God to others, but about discovering that unique revelation of God that each person is.

- Being evangelized ourselves means that we become aware of our uniqueness and of the presence of God within us. This in turn leads us to discover how original and amazing every other person is and how splendid and dignified is the whole of creation. This will transform the way we treat other people and how we use creation.
- Evangelizing others is sensitive work. It means helping an individual toward a spiritual awakening in which they begin to see themselves as God created them.

I believe this true sense of evangelization is something we have to take very seriously if the good news is to be awakened in people today.

In our modern, fragmented, and externalist society, a precondition for evangelization will be the creation of silence and a return to inwardness and reflection. This is the real coming home. That is why I have suggested that in using this book, it is important to spend time over the chapter contents as well as over the Scripture reflection and prayer.

I would like to end with a verse that I came across some years ago on a bookmark. In a simple way it sums up the heart of evangelization and what this book has tried to do.

What greater joy can a person experience
than to help others become aware
of the love,
the truth,
and the splendor
residing in their hearts...
that each person is a reflection of God's goodness.

About the Author

Peter Verity is a Roman Catholic priest in Cumbria, England, and former Director of the Catholic Media Office in London. He worked as editor of the London Catholic Missionary Society magazine *Catholic Gazette*, and currently serves as chair of the Diocesan Education Commission and Diocesan Trustee.